Mike Gardner's

FISH HAVE NO HANDS

CATCHING TONS OF FISH IN BAYS AND ESTUARIES

The gods do not deduct from man's allotted span the hours spent in fishing.

—*Babylonian proverb*

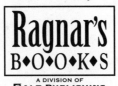

Ragnar's
B◆O◆O◆K◆S
A DIVISION OF
GALT PUBLISHING

800/400-0890

TABLE OF CONTENTS

FISH HAVE NO HANDS

FOREWORD

The first time I saw Mike Gardner, he was hoisting a large, legal halibut onto his boat. He was pictured in a newspaper profile regaling Mike and his technique for catching big numbers of fish near-shore, particularly in bays and estuaries.

Having just moved to the Newport Bay area, and being a lifelong angler, I was more than a little interested in having someone show me the hot spots in the bay, and how best to fish them. I was particularly interested in catching keeper halibut, since that's one trophy that had eluded me.

I got my first inkling of what I was in for when Mike told me over the telephone, "On a bad day, we catch fifty to one hundred fish. On a good day, we get two hundred fifty to three hundred."

A bad day was fifty fish? I scheduled a trip for my wife and I on the spot, and couldn't even begin to fathom the idea of three people pulling three hundred fish into the boat.

When you fish with Mike, you're on the dock at 6AM, on the water shortly thereafter, and fishing before you know it. At Newport, we'd barely motored away from the dock when Mike stopped to demonstrate how we'd be fishing that day, using the method he's perfected over a life-time of fishing.

It started with his patented, intriguing "grab your shirt between your thumb and forefinger and pull it one-quarter inch away from your chest. That's a bite." He then walked us through each step of his method, casting toward some vegetation along the shoreline. He caught fish on each of his first three casts. Impressive.

He also casually pointed out along the way that his name was on the rods we were fishing with, and not the same way you or I might scrawl our names on our stuff to show it's ours. No, these were Lamiglas Mike Gardner In-Shore Pro Rods, manufactured with Mike's name right on them. *Very* impressive. And darn fine rods, to boot.

The rest of that day Mike showed us why Lamiglas manufactures rods with his name right on them: He's an incredible fisherman.

We had somewhat tied his hands that day, first by insisting on fishing Newport Bay when the action was considerably better in some of the other local bays, and second, our inexperience with baitcasters (to put it nicely), but Mike was more than up to the challenge.

It wasn't one of those fantasy trips everyone dreams of, where every cast is bit and the challenge is to get your fish to the boat before another fish eats him, but it was the most enjoyable day of fishing we'd ever had. My wife, Lisa, who had only been out on party boats in saltwater and who **hates** getting up early, had a particularly good time.

Even though it was a "slow" day, and my wife and I caught a surprising number of fish, and we mangled Mike's method. Mike, on the other hand, caught quite a few fish. More than I'd ever seen anyone catch. He caught fish where I was sure there weren't any, and got bites when I thought I was getting nothing.

It was about the best demonstration of a perfected technique you could ask for, and, being in the publishing business, we thought, "This would make a great book." We hope you agree.

I've learned more about fishing by working with Mike over the past few months than I had in years of throwing lines in rivers, lakes and the ocean. The most surprising part was the versatility of the knowledge. Mike is teaching specifically for near-shore, bay and estuary fishing, but what he's teaching can be applied to almost any kind of fishing you do.

I've used Mike's tips and tricks to improve my results fishing for dorado on a full-day boat out of San Diego, as well as trout fishing in Central Oregon. I also catch quite a few fish in Newport Bay and, to be honest, I still haven't mastered Mike's technique completely, but I do see a real difference between my results and those of anglers I talk to on the shore.

Recently I was talking to a guy who's been fishing Newport for nearly ten years, and wasn't catching nearly as many fish as I was. One thing he mentioned was how often he got "broke off," which is part of the game when you're fishing around structure.

I bounced three or four questions off of him about why his line might be breaking, and he'd never considered any of them. Until I met Mike, I hadn't thought of them either.

I also didn't really understand why fish are where they are, why they like to hit a lure, when they like to hit a lure, and what tricks I can use to give me just that little extra edge that can make the difference between landing a fish and catching a fish story.

Since then, I've been out with Mike a number of times, and I no longer have trouble fathoming catching three hundred fish between three people in one day. In fact, he's got me a little spoiled, because I used to think I'd done really well if I'd caught fifteen or twenty fish in a day. Now I look at that many fish as just getting started.

But the best part has been getting to know Mike. As I think you'll find, Mike is one of those people who's just larger than life. During a day on the water with him, you'll hear stories you won't believe, and even more that you will. If you have the opportunity to hire Mike for a trip, do it, because there's only so much room for his personality in this book, and there are large chunks of it I would never even *consider* printing.

I still haven't landed my keeper halibut, but now I know it's just a matter of time. I have caught a ton of spotted bay bass, a bunch of sand bass, a good number of halibut (up to eighteen inches—so close), some calico bass, a big sculpin, a bat ray and a few things that, frankly, I don't know what they were. I've also been unfortunate enough to catch a sea gull (who, luckily, threw the hook) and a sailboat (that I was never able to get to the net), so when Mike tells you that you never know what you'll catch in the bays, believe him. And you'd be amazed how hard a sailboat fights.

If you're one of those people who thinks you've got to pay big bucks to be elbow-to-elbow on a cattle boat to catch fish, prepare to be surprised. If you've always wondered if there were fish in that bay or harbor and what kind, you're about to find out, and you're going to like the answer. And if you've often questioned just what it would take for you to catch fish near-shore and in bays and estuaries, get ready to learn answers that will dramatically change your fishing, and your *catching*.

Greg Compton
Publisher

INTRODUCTION

I guess you could say I was born to be a fisherman. I've been fishing since I was a toddler in Naples, California, where I got many a spanking for going down to the water without the big guys.

We lived five houses from the canal, and the grammar school was across the street from me. Behind the grammar school was the bay. I was half a block from the bay and a half a block from the canal.

When we later moved to Los Angeles, I started making my dad take my brother and I fishing at Pierpoint Landing. Fortunately for us, he had a store in Santa Monica, so he would take us to the pier and leave us all day. During the summer, I got a job as a pinhead on the barge—big deal, a kid on a barge. When I was sixteen, I'd go out on the sport boats as a pinhead and as a deck hand. I was always working, I always had a job. And I loved fishing. Always have and I always will.

Saltwater fishing was my thing. Then, back in the early sixties, my brother got into freshwater fishing at Irvine Lake with a friend of ours that we went to school with. And my brother kept telling me, "You gotta try this, this is great. Bass fishing is wonderful." And I said, "Pete, you're looking for a fish that's the size of what I use for bait."

But I gave in, and went with him one time to Irvine. This was back in the old days, and he gave me a

wimpy old spinning rod that he didn't care whether it got broken or not, and he put a Chub Creek Darter on the end of my line. I'll never forget; it was a Chub CD, which is a wooden surface lure. It was foggy, and I threw it next to this little twig that was sticking up in the water. I was watching the ripples go, and he said, "Now, when the ripples stop, wiggle the lure; just jiggle it." So, I was waiting for the ripples to stop, and about a two-pound bass came streaking up and flew out of the water with my lure in its mouth, and I was hooked just as hard. Right then and there I became a freshwater bass fanatic.

From that day on, I was into it, and in 1968 and '69, I was talking to a guy that ran one of the local sporting goods stores about starting a bass club. My brother was a member of the South Bay Bass Masters, and there were only a few bass clubs in the state of California. There was Southern California Bass Masters, South Bay Bass Masters, Saddleback Bass Masters and I think West Valley had started one. I said, "Let's start our own," because my brother had said, "I'm not letting you in mine." And we did.

We started Rio Hondo Bass Masters, the first bass club in the Whittier area, and we organized inter-club tournaments. At the same time, a friend and I decided to start a fishing "insurance" program. It worked like this: If you caught a fish over a certain size, big enough to mount, whether it be a largemouth bass, a catfish, a crappie, a bluegill, anything that was considered a mountable fish, we would pay to mount it, if you paid a $12 a year insurance fee. What a great idea.

In order to publicize our brainstorm, we started a team tournament concept called the California Lunker Club. You paid two bucks a person, four dollars a team, and we held these tournaments once or twice a month all over Southern California in all these different lakes. This is where tournament bass fishing in the West actually got its start. It became very successful as far as attracting the anglers, and very unsuccessful as far as us making any money. Because every time we turned around, someone caught a fish, a bass over eight pounds or some other whopper, and it would cost us $150 to mount it, and that's all we'd made in the tournament. So we never got ahead. But we did do a lot of fishing, and that's never changed.

I can safely say that if you counted a lifetime of more than fifty years of fishing, I've probably caught over half a million fish, which is quite an accomplishment when you look at it through the eyes of an angler. Think about that for a minute. Half a million fish. 500,000. That's a lot of fishing, and, more important, a lot of catching. You may hear a guy say, "I've caught thousands of fish," but if you really stopped and had him think about it, tally it up, he probably didn't catch that many.

But if you want to put up the really big numbers yourself, I'm willing to show you how. Part of the secret is concentrating on saltwater, near-shore. In freshwater, sometimes I would go out and only catch five or six fish in a day. Then I would get those exceptional days, which are pretty rare, when I would catch fifty, sixty, a hundred fish in a day. But those are really rare days in freshwater.

In saltwater, on the other hand, a rare day for me is a day when I drop *below* a hundred fish. Sometimes, in places like San Diego Bay, we catch two hundred and fifty to three hundred fish in one day. It's not a fair comparison between freshwater and saltwater. It's apples and oranges, but I've found I've developed quite a taste for oranges.

I can tell you stories about how the wardens used to come up to my boat and my customers would tell them, "We've caught more than two hundred fifty fish today." The warden would think they were lying and climb in the boat and say, "Let's see them."

"Well, we released them all except for a limit apiece." There would be four of us in the boat. And he would look in the live well and see forty fish. It would blow him away, because he hadn't seen anybody with that many fish. So, yeah, I do catch a lot of fish, and it's not by accident.

Ironically, one of the things that got me interested in near-shore fishing was the freshwater fishing. I developed a method. I learned from other people in freshwater fishing to use light lures and a light line, and small reaction baits, small little plastic baits, do-nothing baits. I realized you could catch a ton of fish, if the fish thought it was an easy meal.

I developed a method when I was fishing tournaments. I used little, small quarter-ounce lead-headed jigs and a four-inch, purple Mister Twister Phenom worm, rigged with an open hook. And I would throw it against walls and structure in open water or areas where it was unlikely to get snagged. And I caught lots and lots of fish. And I won my share of tournaments.

I started guiding in 1973, because the I.R.S. didn't recognize professional bass fishing as a sport. I had to pay taxes on the money I won, but I couldn't deduct my expenses. So my accountant says, "Be a guide. Get a guide's license, start being a guide, take people fishing on the pre-fish days and you can write off every trip, including the

tournaments, because you're practicing to be a guide." So that's exactly what I did.

I started guiding on freshwater, and when I got so busy that I couldn't always go to freshwater, I would go to Newport Bay and I would practice, using that very same method, with the light lures, and the light, six-pound test line. And down there I'd catch two hundred fish in one day. It was easy, dynamite.

That's how I got into this. Of course, I refined my technique, and refined my technique and developed this method, with a lot of help from other professional fisherman, who I used to practice with, to finally arrive at this simple—very simple—way of working these lures.

Like most things in life, there's no big, big secret. It's doing all the little things right. It's the fishermen who do all the little things right that eventually catch the majority of the fish. You know the old saw about, "Ten percent of the fishermen catch ninety percent of the fish." That's true. I've seen it a number of different ways, but it's true. A small percentage of the fishermen have the knowledge and are doing the right thing in the right place.

I've spent my whole life fishing the waters in and around Southern California, and you'll hear me refer to local fishing spots throughout this book. But don't think my method only works in Southern California, because you'd be wrong. This method knocks 'em dead in bays and estuaries, period. I've tried it in Hawaii, I've tried it in Louisiana, I've tried it in Texas, and the only difference was the fish on the end of the hook. I may be saying Newport Bay, but you can substitute the name of your local bay and expect similar results. Where I'm catching spotted bay bass, you may be catching redfish. Bunches of them.

There are certain basic principles that will allow you to become a far superior fisherman than your friends. If you adhere to the basic principles and techniques I demonstrate and recognize certain basic facts that I'm going to explain, you can become that superior fisherman. I've spent years perfecting my techniques; these are tried and true methods.

Now, all through this book, you will hear me saying, if there is any secret to what I do in near-shore fishing, it's light, six-pound test line. Or lighter. Sometimes I use four-pound line. And sometimes I use eight-pound test for the bigger fish and out in more open waters. But in the bays and estuaries, I am a firm believer in four- and six-pound test.

Well, I suppose there is one other secret, and that's probably the most important thing we'll discuss—recognizing a pressure strike, the most subtle of subtle strikes. To know when the fish has a lure in his mouth—he doesn't have it in his hands. **Fish have no hands.** It's in his mouth. And it's in his mouth far more often than you think it is.

One of the first things I tell my clients during a guide trip is "take hold of your shirt between your thumb and forefinger, and pull it one-quarter inch away from your chest. That's a bite." And it's that subtle. Miss it, and you'll never know a fish was there. Learn to recognize it, and you'll be on your way.

You'll catch so many fish once you've mastered this method, compared to what you have been doing, that you won't believe it. Guys tell me all the time, "Well, we had a pretty good day today. We caught five or six fish down there. We caught a halibut and six bass and we really did good." To them, that's a good day.

For me, I would commit *hari-kari*. There would be a *seppuku* ceremony right on the bow of my boat if I did that badly. That's five minutes'

worth of fishing. I was out recently with Marty Millner, from the *Let's Talk Hook-up* radio show, in San Diego Bay. While he was rigging his rod, I put ten fish into the boat. *While he was rigging his rod.* We caught over two hundred fifty fish that day, and we only fished from ten until three. Five hours. And it was supposed to be a bad day in San Diego. We even spent a lot of time moving around because we got tired of just sitting in one place. We could have stayed in that one spot all day and we would have just killed them. Yes, catching tons of fish in bays and estuaries is not a remote possibility with this method, it's a likely possibility.

When I take my customers fishing, I'm always fishing. I'm not the type of guide who's just a cross between a chauffeur and a gondolier, who says, "Let's try here, maybe you'll catch something." A day on the water with me is a full day of fishing and learning about fishing, and I teach by example as well as by word. I tell my clients how to do it, tell them how it works, and then show them that it works. I'll use the same approach in this book, using lots of photos to illustrate what I'm telling

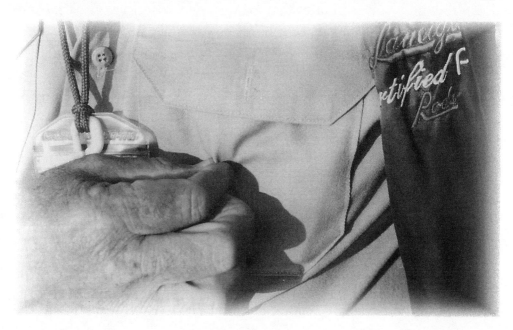

you in the text. Follow along, look at the photos, and take this book fishing with you.

We're going to talk in detail about learning this method, the different facets of tackle, of technique, and using all of the factors that become a whole to make this method of fishing amazingly effective. It's not just one thing. There is no magic. It's the combination of doing all the little things right that make it an effective method.

There are little tips and tricks in fishing that are almost always learned by trial and error. Most anglers reading this book are learning little things in a few hour's worth of reading that took me a lifetime to learn and perfect. It's just like tournament bass fishing. When I became a professional during the old days of bass fishing, I learned all these things about structure fishing and using sonar when there wasn't sonar and finding the different depths and so forth the hard way.

Now, there's all kinds of scientific equipment. There are all kinds of top-notch rods and reels, and lures that are extremely effective. The trial and error of fishing, the majority of it has been explained in books and movies and videos and on TV. And most anglers have the benefit of learning this stuff that took us old-timers years and years and years to

learn. Sometimes anglers are looking for big, giant revelations. There are no big giant revelations.

What makes you a pro fisherman? Does some guy touch you on

each shoulder with a rod that has eighty-four inches of diamond wrap on it, and that makes you a pro? After all, eighty-four inches of diamond wrap means it has to be a pro rod, right? Nobody really knows for sure. But we do

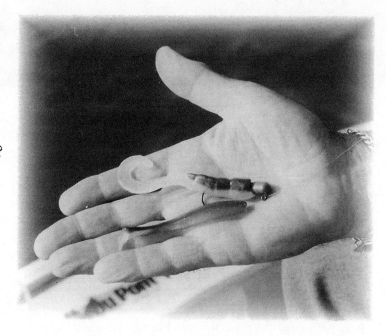

know that there are certain tricks and techniques in fishing that have been discovered by guys doing them over and over again, and catching lots of fish. And the pros catch lots of fish.

Therefore, these are little pearls of wisdom that are coming your way. I have perfected a technique of my own that yields tremendous results, and if you follow closely, and take the time to master these techniques, you can turn your good fishing days into days you never thought possible. But always keep this in mind: *Fish Have No Hands.*

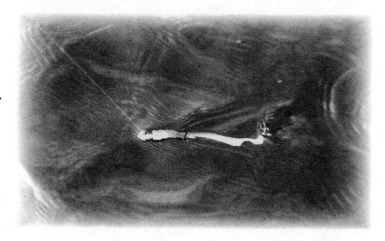

FISH WHERE *1* THE FISH ARE

Fish are all over the place near-shore, in bays, estuaries and harbors. A lot of people go out and spend a fortune taking a boat ride. It always cracks me up to see people leave the harbor and go flat-out as soon as they hit the end of the five-mile-an-hour buoy. They floor the boat and go straight out—eight hundred yards, half a mile, a mile—and stop the boat and start fishing.

For what earthly reason are they fishing there? There's absolutely nothing in that spot. They didn't see any birds working; there's no structure; there's no big, deep drop-off. There's no reason, other than it looked like a good spot and the guy decided to stop. Then he's the one who comes in and says, "Fishing was terrible. They weren't biting at all today." When in reality the guy who's fishing structure or where the fish are or where the birds are working is going to hammer them and come in with tons of fish, while Mr. Boat Ride has nothing.

You have to learn to fish where the fish are. That is essential. One of the biggest reasons I catch more fish than everybody else is that I fish where the fish are the majority of the time.

I am one of the ten percent of the people that catch ninety percent of the fish because I am where the fish are ninety-nine percent of the time.

Now, that's not to say I didn't spend my share of time fishing where the fish weren't. I may have been born to be a fisherman, but I wasn't born a pro. I had to work on that. I had my days when the fishing was just lousy, when I'd pray, "Please Lord just one. I can't go in with an empty stringer," and I'd be cursing the tides, the water, the light, the barometric pressure, the fish and the gasoline in my tank.

I'd pull up to the dock, still muttering, when a boat would pull up next to me and guys would start handing out huge stringers of fish. "Where'd you get those?" I'd roar. "In the water." "On what?" "A hook." Jerks. As if I didn't feel bad enough about a stinker of a day, I needed that kind of needling on top of it?

One thing it did teach me was to share everything I know with anyone who wants to learn. Ask me where I caught my fish—I'll tell you. Ask me what lure I'm using—I'll tell you. They're probably AA's curly tail grubs, and there's a good chance I'll even give you a few.

When I was teaching for the National Bass Fishing Institute, I learned that in any given body of fresh water, only four to six percent has fish life of any specie in it. The rest of the water is devoid of

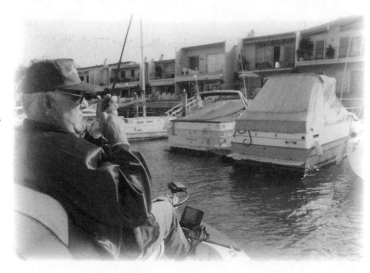

fish. Whether it's anoxic water (water lacking sufficient oxygen for fish life), whether it's below the thermocline—for any number of reasons—it doesn't have fish in it.

If you're looking specifically for largemouth bass in a lake, and all kinds of different fish are in the lake—crappie, bluegill, catfish, stripers—but you want largemouth bass, less than one percent of the lake will have largemouth bass in it. So you're looking in that lake for largemouth bass, and you've only got one percent of the lake that has those fish in it. Of that big volume of water, whether it's a lake, a river, a stream, less than one percent. Not great odds.

In saltwater, the odds are astronomically worse than one percent. They're maybe one-tenth of one percent. If you're looking for, say calico bass, in one little teeny area, they have miles and miles and miles of water to hide in, nearly all of which is devoid of fish life. You have to know where the fish are, where they hang out, what attracts them. Why fish are where they are.

In most bays and estuaries, the lay up of land is usually very shallow. They generally have beaches, and they usually have a drop-off in them

for a channel, and very, very little natural structure. Most of the structure is man-made. There are bays that have pilings, that have drop-offs, that have retaining walls, that have shade created from moored boats. Boats are moored to buoys and the buoys have an old car engine block, or a big cement block that's holding it in place with a chain running up to the buoy or a rope that is encrusted with barnacles and so forth. That's the only structure; therefore, that's where the fish will be.

Fish relate to structure. They'll be up against the steep walls. They'll be against the pilings and against the drop-offs, and they're almost always on the shady side. Fish like the shady side of structure not because the light hurts their eyes, as many people think, but because they feel more secure in the low light.

Keep in mind that fish don't live in a nice, cultured society— they live in a wet jungle. A fish

Structure in bays and harbors comes in many varieties, and it's usually man-made.

doesn't reach any kind of maturity by being reckless. Reckless fish are lunch. So the careful fish keep to where it's hard for them to be seen, which means the shady side of structure.

I've found that in bays, estuaries and harbors, the fish have certain characteristics which are pretty basic. They're going to relate to structure of some sort or another, as I've said.

Each species has characteristics that are inherent to just that species. Everyone used to think halibut just liked to lay around on the sand. Yes, they do like to lay around on the sand, but they also want to be next to structure that attracts bait fish—next to eel grass, next to rocks, in the sand next to the rocks. Also, halibut will find an area, and it will be like a halibut hotel. There will be bunch of halibut there. They don't school, but they do group.

Fish relate to structure, so don't overlook anything in the bay that could provide them with shelter or protection. As a rule, they'll be on the shady side.

Spotted bay bass are the same way. They don't school, but they will collect in small groups in areas they find appealing. They'll be by themselves next to a twig, but at the next twig over, there might be another one, because they all like that particular structure. In bays and estuaries the spotted bay bass like the engine blocks that hold down the buoys by the pilings.

But at certain times of the year, the fish will be up shallow; at other times of year, they're down deep. In the summertime, they're in two places. The ones that have spawned or are waiting to spawn are up shallow in the eel grass. The ones that are about to spawn are in real deep water in a spawning aggregation, where there's a giant cluster of fish.

Spotted bay bass are broadcast spawners. In other words, they don't bear live young. The females lay their eggs, and the males fertilize their eggs. This happens on the full moon. They'll be out there waiting near the time of the full moon. In San Diego Bay, you can get

Spotted bay bass are one of the most common species in Southern California bays, harbors and estuaries, and one of the most fun to catch.

tons of 'em out in deep water, because the fish will be out there waiting to spawn.

Spotties don't pair off like largemouth bass do, where you get a pair and they make a little nest and everything. When the female spotties start laying eggs, the males get excited and shoot milt. The two meet and you have fertilized eggs. Those eggs go out in the water column, leaving the bay or estuary, and the current will take them out to sea. The eggs will hatch, they'll stay in the plankton, and then the fish will swim back into a bay or estuary. A fish that was born in San Diego may end up in Oceanside, because of the current.

Calico bass are most likely to be found near shore and around the breakwater rather than in the bays and harbors, but if there's good, hard structure, there's a chance they'll be around.

Spotted bay bass love eel grass; they love shallower water; and they love bays and estuaries. Very rarely will you find a spotted bay bass in the open ocean. Very rarely.

You do find spotted bay bass in Avalon Harbor, and as far north as Marina Del Rey, with an occasional one or two in Oxnard, but the water gets cooler as it goes north, and spotted bay bass are a semi-tropical fish. You won't find them in San Francisco, for example, or Monterey. You'll find them mostly down through the tip of Baja.

Calico bass like structure, hard structure, such as rocks, submerged pilings or a rock pile. You don't usually find calicos on ledges or drop-offs. You'll find them against a breakwater, against a retaining wall. They also like to be in the kelp, which is why, no surprise here, they're also called kelp bass. They'll suspend in among the stringers, waiting for food to float by. Very rarely will you ever find a calico bass in eel grass.

Sand bass relate to the bottom. If they're on the Long Beach breakwater, for example, they'll be at the bottom of a wall, in a group. They do congregate in big schools though, in giant schools of sand bass.

If someone were to ask me what my very favorite nearshore species to fish for is, I'd say, hands down, it's the spotted bay bass. It's the meanest little critter that ever lived. Of the three species of saltwater nearshore bass, calico or kelp bass, barred sand bass and the spotted bay bass, the spotted bay bass is, without a doubt, the meanest.

Barred sand bass are also commonly found in the bays. Sand bass, as their name suggests, like sandy bottoms, and will school in large groups.

The spottie is also the best fighter, with the calico coming in a close second, and then the sand bass bringing up the rear—the lowly sand bass that just lays there. But you can get some big ones that will give you a fight. I like catching halibut, I love catching spot fin croaker, and yellow fin croaker and white sea bass, but my very favorite fish is the spotted bay bass. Why? Because of the mere tenacity of the fish.

Halibut come in all sizes, including extra-small like this one. Be sure to handle small fish gently, to increase their chances of survival when you release them. It will be a few years before this guy's big enough to keep.

With a largemouth bass, when I used to fish largemouth, you have a habit of grabbing the fish by the lower jaw, and it's paralyzed. Well, when you grab a spotted bay bass by the lower jaw, he's pissed. And he climbs up your finger trying to eat all the way from the tip of your thumb to your knuckle.

They never stop fighting, never. Other fish stop, get tired; a spotted bay bass will fight until you kill him or put him back in the water. They're the meanest little critters around. And they have sharp teeth. You can reach over the teeth to remove the hook, but that doesn't mean you're not going to get bit. And you'll know when you're bit.

The characteristics of these fish are very important, and you should learn the characteristics of the species you are looking for. If you're fishing outside of Southern California, do a little research on what species are native to your bays and harbors, and their tendencies. The more you know, the more fish you'll catch.

I've fished my method in the Gulf of Mexico, in Louisiana and Texas, for redfish and drum and found it extremely deadly. They're bigger fish, but they hit the artificial lures in exactly the same way. We'll talk a little later about the pressure bite and using a different type of plastic bait

The sculpin is one of the tastiest fish you'll find in the bays, but they're rattlesnakes. Their spines are poisonous, and they use them to paralyze their prey. If you get stung by one of these, even after the fish is dead, you'll get a serious lesson in pain.

(they may like a different color), but the presentation and the methodology are the same and just as effective, whether it be here or on the Gulf Coast.

When I fished Hawaii, I couldn't name one fish except the bonito, but they were fish. All I know is they all had teeth and they were funny looking, and we caught hundreds of fish in a couple of days of fishing in Lahaina Harbor. People were blown away because they had never seen anybody catch that many fish. We caught every kind there was on artificial lures, using my method. The skipper of the marlin boat that we were on—we were going to go out to catch marlin—stayed there for an hour while I caught these fish, and wanted to use my rod. So it works all over.

While not as common as their cousins, it's not all that unusual to find a white sea bass on the end of your lure.

But most of the time the species I target are the basses: spotted bay bass, calico, sand bass. We also get a number of flat fish, such as halibut, soles and turbot, as well as some spot and yellow fin croaker and rays.

And, of course, there's white sea bass in the bays, as well as young of virtually every species: barracuda, bonito, mackerel, sculpin, perch, not to mention the bait fish, such as smelt and anchovies. You never know what you'll find in the bays, harbors and estuaries.

As a rule, you want to focus on the specie that is most predominant in your area, because fishing for the most common specie will naturally increase the number of fish you're likely to catch.

Moving Water Means Feeding Fish

One of the things we're going to talk about are the moon phases and the tides. How the moon affects the tides, and how the tides affect the fishing. Moving water means feeding fish. On the days when you have lousy tides and the astro tables or moon phase tables tell you it will be bad fishing, it will probably be bad fishing. And on the days when it tells you that it will be good fishing, you can still have bad fishing. There are a number of variables: A storm comes through; you have a sudden drop in barometric pressure; your boat catches fire. A lot of things can happen, most of them bad. But if you know what you're doing, what you call a bad day could be another guy's good day.

Look for the times when you have large quantities of water movement, and, of course, low light conditions, and those will be your best fishing times.

When you have lots of water moving in the morning and evening, that's your best time to fish. Low light penetration is always better than high light penetration, for those fish security reasons I mentioned. And you'll do better to fish in the

Moving water means feeding fish, and the faster the water's moving, the better your chances for a bite.

early morning or at the last light of the day. The wives always say, "Why did you have to be there first thing in the morning," or, "Why did you have to come home so late?" Because, honey, that's when the fish were biting.

TODAY'S CATCH IS TOMORROW'S LUNKER

I am a one hundred percent believer in catch and release to help preserve, and hopefully increase, the native population of fish in bays and estuaries. Take only what you'll eat. Newport Bay here in Southern California is a prime example. We used to go down there and catch two or three hundred fish in one day; now if we catch a hundred fish, we're extremely lucky. There is currently some pressure to have the Department of Fish and Game (DFG) declare a moratorium on taking spotted bay bass from the bay, or at least to develop a smaller number limit.

The breeder fish have been taken out of Newport Bay. There was very poor recruitment out of there for a number years—poor recruitment meaning low levels of spawning and survival of the young—of almost all the species in Newport Bay.

The more fish that you release today, the more fish there will be for you to catch tomorrow.

One of the reasons is that Newport Bay is fed by the Santa Ana River, which carries nutrients that are washed into the bay. This runoff turns the water into a stained, off-color, and brings nutrients into the bay. Moss is created, and algae is created, off of which the bait fish feed and thrive, and the game fish feed on the bait fish.

But then we had a drought. We went through a period when, for years, there was no water coming into the bay. The water in the bay became crystal clear, and all the eel grass died off, the kelp died off and the algae died off. It's just like quail eggs and water. If there's no water, the quail have a bad hatch. It's the same way with the bass and other fish species. If there's no cover for the young, no eel grass for the small fish to take cover in, they either get eaten or they don't spawn as much.

On top of that, some of the anglers I've taught how to catch all these fish have literally raped Newport Bay, and they caught the spawners. Therefore, there is not as much recruitment and not as much spawning and survival—it's a vicious circle.

Dr. Larry Allen, of the California State University, Northridge, Near-Shore Marine Fisheries Program, believes that all in-shore bays and

It takes years for spotted bay bass to replenish themselves. If you don't plan on eating them right away, put 'em back in, so they can live to fight another day.

estuaries are cyclical, and that this stage at Newport is just part of the cycle. Therefore, he feels there will be better survival and better spawn in the next few years. The spawn has been pretty good lately, so we'll see what happens.

Catch and release is critical for the long-term survival of these species, particularly when you're catching as many fish as I'll teach you to catch. And there is a proper way and an improper way to catch and release fish.

The most important consideration for properly releasing fish is to preserve the protective slime that covers his body. Scraping the slime off a fish is like removing the skin from your body. The epidermal layer of your body protects your flesh, and it keeps you from getting infections.

The same thing applies to the slime on a fish. The slime on a fish protects it from getting infections. Those people who have tropical fish tanks know that if they handle their fish and it removes the slime, the fish gets an infection and dies. Saltwater or freshwater, if you take the slime off a fish, he'll act very lively. But after you release him, he'll get an infection and die, so what have you accom-

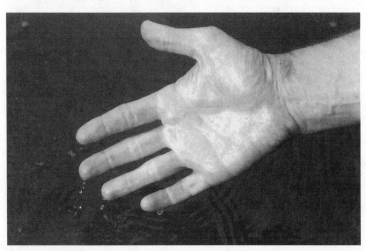

Never handle a fish with dry hands or a dry towel, it will remove the protective slime from his body, he'll get an infection, and die. Always wet your hands before touching the fish.

plished by releasing him?

In bass tournaments, we found that out the hard way. Guys were keeping fish on stringers, they were keeping fish in live wells, but they were handling the fish at weigh-in time and the fish would

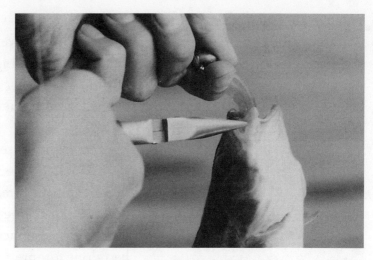

Handle any fish you intend to release as little as possible. If you can remove the hook without touching him at all, that's ideal.

lose their slime. They would send divers down at the release sites at tournaments and they'd find lots of dead fish in the tournament area. Same thing in saltwater. We were finding fish that were dying after they'd been released. People thought they were letting them go, but they would handle them, they would drop them on the deck, and they'd effectively kill them before putting them back in the water.

Always wet your hands before handling a fish, and if you have to use a rag, be sure to use a wet rag. With calico bass, sand bass and spotted bay bass, I reach in the fish's mouth over its teeth with my forefinger and thumb and remove the hook and let the fish go. If you can't remove the hook, if it's in the gullet, cut the line, the hook will rot out. But cut the monofilament right up against the hook, or as close as you can, and let it go.

If you use a net, it is quite possible that your net will harm the fish. If the net is made of the wrong material, it can scrape the slime off the fish.

Halibut are especially tricky. For years I thought I was letting thousands of little halibut go that were under the legal limit (twenty-two inches in California). I thought I was doing the world such a big favor. Then one day I was out with Chuck Garrison from *South Coast Sportfishing* magazine. I caught a small halibut and scooped it in my net.

Be particularly careful in handling halibut. If you can land the small ones without a net, do it. If you must use a net, be sure it's a fine mesh net.

He showed me a picture that ran in his magazine of a small halibut with his tail split in three places between the mesh of the net—split to the quick. He explained to me that he had done an interview with the halibut research people at Cal State Northridge and from hub Sea World, and he found out that many of the halibut that were caught during the annual Halibut Derby in Santa Monica Bay and were tagged, died in the tanks because their tails had been split. They got infections and died. This netting mesh problem is not a concern for the bass species, but it's deadly for halibut.

What you need for halibut is a small-mesh net. Very small mesh, the same mesh that you would use for anchovies. But many of the people that catch these small halibut, by the time they've bounced them on the deck, taking all the slime off of them, it doesn't matter if they netted them or not—they're going to die. If you want to prevent your released halibut from dying, get the right net and leave the slime on the fish. It's an important thing, and it's your responsibility as an angler.

I am not the kind of guy who says don't keep fish for food. If you're going to keep them and eat them, that's fine, enjoy. But don't bring an over-limit home. If you want to bring a limit home, my motto is take only what you're going to eat, and only what you're going to eat that next meal. You don't need to bring home a supply that you're going to keep in the freezer for the next six years that will be ruined by freezer burn before you can get around to eating it. And you don't have to feed the whole neighborhood. The fewer fish that end up in your trash can, the more fish there'll be the next time you go fishing. There's no need to rape the ocean.

One other thing, everybody has a favorite spot. Out in the ocean, fish move around. In bays and estuaries, fish move around, but there's always certain areas where fish hang out. Certain pilings, certain cor-

Good spots are only good as long as you don't fish them out. If you over-fish a spot, it may be years before it recovers.

ners, where there's a lot of moving water, bridges, the bases of bridges and so forth. If you find an area with a large amount of fish and you continually go back to it over and over again, three days a week, keeping the fish, pretty soon you'll have fished it out.

Fish don't replenish themselves anywhere near as readily as people think they do. It takes time for fish to grow. Calico bass, according to the DFG, take approximately four and one-half to five years to grow to twelve inches, depending on the environment.

In some areas, fish grow more quickly than in others. Maybe they have better food, or the water is warmer more often so they are more active—fish are cold-blooded creatures. Sand bass grow relatively quickly. In four years, they're usually around twelve inches.

Fish, like this sand bass, don't get to be a catchable size overnight, and they struggle every day. By the time you catch one of these, he's make it through years of trying to eat without being eaten, before he made the mistake of chomping your lure. Think hard before you take him home; if you're not going to eat him, put him back in the water.

Spotted bay bass, which everybody thought took

nine years to grow to twelve inches, are just the opposite. They're almost dead by the time they're nine. They have an accelerated growth rate, and grow very fast, for fish. By the time they're two years old, they're easily twelve inches. Then, their growth rate levels off, and a two-, two-and-one-half- to three-pound spotted bay bass is a very big spottie. Any spotted bay bass over four pounds is a mountable fish.

There's no telling what you'll find on the end of your line. I've caught bat rays up to 85 pounds in the bays. Just because you don't intend to keep the fish, or it wasn't what you were after, is no excuse for mistreating a fish. Oh, and watch out for that stinger.

Usually, spotted bay bass die at around thirteen to fourteen years of age. That's the oldest one we've been able to verify through studies. The spottie is a fish that can be fished out very quickly. It's not like calico bass, where you can find one that's thirty-five years old and weighs fifteen pounds. They're never going to be that way.

All species should be treated with respect. Don't kill it unless you're going to eat it. I see guys catching bat rays and sharks and they say, "Eh, throw it up on the bank, it's just a shark." Hey, that's nature—you don't need to kill it. If you're not going to eat it, don't kill it.

YOU GONNA EAT THAT?

No one wants to glow in the dark and no one wants to be pregnant and have a child that looks like a thalidomide baby. Make sure the area you're fishing is safe to eat the fish from.

Usually, the really bad areas have posted warnings, but not always. Sometimes it's hard to find out. For instance, in our research we found that the fish in San Diego Bay were almost toxic, they were so highly polluted. (Sailor, don't eat that fish.)

On the other hand, in Newport Bay, where everybody thought the fish were inedible because the bay was polluted, it turned out that the bay is flushing itself, and the fish are all right to eat.

It's always a good idea to check out an area before you decide to eat the fish. When in doubt, throw it back.

There are certain areas where the fishing may be good, but the eating isn't really recommended. Fish, like most animals, tend to develop a taste based on what they've been eating. If you're going to fish on the sewer line, for example, I don't think you're going to like the taste of that fish. There are certain common sense areas where cities dump sewage and so forth where you just don't want to eat the fish.

Off of Point Fermin, Palos Verdes, where LA dumps sewage, for instance. They tell you, if

There's no telling what can contaminate the water you're fishing in—sewage, heavy metals, you name it. A good fishing spot could have toxic fish and you might never know it. You'll never get sick by not eating a fish, but the first time you get sick from the fish that was contaminated you'll never take that chance again. Most waters are fine to take fish from, but nearly all water is polluted to some extent. Make the effort to check it out before you eat the fish you catch.

you're pregnant, don't eat more than so many of these fish. By the Vincent Thomas Bridge in Long Beach Harbor, there's a sign with a skull and crossbones that says don't eat the fish here, it's poisonous. Right by the Dow Chemical plant in the Cerritos Channel. You don't want to eat those fish—you'll light the dial on your watch. So you definitely want to make sure that these things are clear.

Call the DFG office and ask if it's safe to eat the fish in a certain area. They are about the only ones that will tell you, unless you want to call one of the local universities' biology departments that has ichthyologists, and they might be able to tell you. Again, the basic rule is play it safe.

Boats can add pollution to a bay in many ways, including gas and oil leaks and illegally dumping their bilge into the water. If you see anyone, boat or angler, polluting the bay, report them to the Harbor Patrol or Coast Guard. The bays are for everyone, and there's no place for the person who abuses them.

Certain fish have intestinal worms. You should develop a habit of gutting halibut right away. Everybody loves halibut, but it has lots and lots of worms in its stomach. And as soon as the fish dies, the worms leave the stomach and start permeating the meat. I remember one time when I put some halibut in the microwave, started it up, and watched the worms coming up out of the meat. That could cure you of eating fish forever.

It's just like beef; you can get a tapeworm from beef, you can get a tapeworm from fish. Prepare your fish properly. Gut your fish right away after it dies and get the worms out of it. Certain worms are extremely deadly. Nematodes. Some fish have them in their flesh, then you eat them, they get into your intestinal tract and they have to operate on you to remove them. Not a nice thought.

Obviously, if the fish has lesions all over it, or if it looks like it's been eaten alive by microbes, don't eat the thing. I'd avoid touching it. Anytime you get a fish that has a slimy, milky look to its fins, is missing portions of its fins or has fin rot really bad, I wouldn't eat that fish. It's always safest to err on the side of caution, so if anything doesn't look right with the fish, there's no reason to eat it. You're not that hungry, believe me.

Watch for posted signs warning about the condition of the water you're fishing in. Keep in mind that the signs may not always be visible from the water.

THE TOOLS 2 OF THE TRADE

Use quality gear. I can't say it any simpler than that. You can occasionally catch big fish on cheap equipment, but if you want to catch a lot of fish on a consistent basis, you'd better have good equipment. Quality gear always pays for itself.

And you need to take care of it. You can have good equipment, but if you don't maintain it, it's going to turn to junk real quick. That goes quadruple-fold in saltwater. Saltwater deteriorates anything: your skin, your boat, your trailer, your wiring, everything. Your reels will fill up with salt if you're not careful and clean them after each time you go out. Salt is an abrasive that will wear away parts and gears in your reels and your equipment, and do it quickly. So take the time and keep your gear clean.

Ladies, it's okay for him to have more than one rod and more than one

reel, because there are different rods and reels for every application. There are rods for spinner baits and for crank baits; for plastic lead-head jigs and for plastic worms; for light tackle and heavy tackle; and fishing deeper

water and shal-
lower water.
Therefore, you
have to have
more than one or
two rods; you
may need four or
five.

I fish, just myself,
with six rods,
lined up, with
different lures
and different outfits and different stuff rigged on those rods. However,
my wife always points out that Nordstrom opens up at ten o'clock. If I
get a new rod and a new reel, she's going to get a new dress or a new
pair of shoes. A lady with a black belt in spending, I assure you, can get
more than her share of paybacks. I have my hobby, she has hers; mine's
fishing, hers is spending.

RODS

I like a lighter action rod. So, when I tell you that six-pound test line is
the secret, don't run out and get a tuna stick and a Penn Squidder reel
and put seven thousand yards of six-pound test on it and go fish
between the docks and the pilings in ten feet of water in Newport Bay.
Use the proper, balanced equipment.

Obviously, I prefer the Mike Gardner In-Shore Pro rod series from
Lamiglas, but not because they offered to put my name on their rods. I
got over having my name on rods years ago. I like the Lamiglas rods
because Lamiglas let me design them for in-shore, bay and estuary fishing, just the way I wanted them.

You don't have to use these particular rods to be successful, but for me, they're optimal. Whatever you choose, make sure it's light. We're using tackle that more closely resembles freshwater outfits than saltwater rigs, and it makes a big difference in the number of fish you'll catch.

For the bays and estuaries, I'm going to use a lighter rod. I usually govern which one of my rod models to use by the water depth. If I'm fishing a lighter lure in shallow water, I'll use a light casting model or a medium-light casting model. If I'm fishing in a little deeper water, like twenty to twenty-five feet, I'll use a medium or medium-light casting rod, and a little bit longer stick, usually a six- to six-and-one-half-footer.

When fishing between the docks and pilings in bays and harbors, I like a five and one-half foot rod. It's short; it's tight. I can make very accurate casts in between the docks and pilings. I'm not casting a million miles, and I want to be able to put my lure exactly where I want it.

This Lamiglas Mike Gardner In-Shore Pro Rod is one of an entire line made especially for near-shore, bay and estuary fishing.

Then when I'm fishing breakwater or real deep water, I'll use six and one-half foot rods. But I'll very rarely go over six and one-half foot when I'm inshore fishing. Now, when I'm outside, in the open ocean, fishing the shoreline, the big breakers and the kelp beds and stuff, I'll use a heavier, seven-foot stick, and I'll be throwing heavier line with bigger plastic baits for calicos, and other large fish. But in the bays and harbors, I like a shorter rod.

I want a rod that has a longer foregrip, either for a baitcaster or a spinner. When you do get a bigger fish on a light rod, the rod tip tends to torque or twist, so I want to have a place to grip the rod in front of the reel, so it doesn't twist. I also like to have a rod with a longer butt, instead of the pistol grip. I don't like a real long butt, but I like the longer butt.

I also like a rod that has a cushioned end. When you bury the rod tip in your chest, around your sternum, if you have that big, hard plastic tip, it hurts. If you catch a lot of fish, by the end of the day you're bruised. I often come back from a good day, where I may personally catch one

hundred twenty five to one hundred fifty fish, and even with the padded new butt tip on the Mike Gardner rods I've got a great big bruise on my chest from catching so many fish. That's not really a problem for me, but for some ladies that might be a great big problem—it really messes up the bikini line.

The good folks at Lamiglas made these rods to my specifications, including features like a longer foregrip and a longer butt. When you're making hundreds of casts and reeling in bunches of fish, these features really make a difference.

I like a rod that has silicon carbine guides for smoothness. When we're using ultralight line, like six-pound test, I want a guide that is real smooth and won't fracture or hurt the line. And while I never want my guides to be wearing down my line, even if I were using rope, it's particularly important with the light line.

Salt's rough on line guides. There are certain tricks that I use when certain things happen. For example, maybe you have the silicon carbide guides I like, and all of a sudden you start getting frayed fishing line and you're breaking off all the time, and it's brand new line. You just put it on. Why is it breaking and why is it frayed? You're not fishing around the rocks. What's the deal?

You probably have a guide that's cracked or split or somebody put a hook in the guide and scarred it up and it's fraying the line. The way I figure that out is, I carry a Q-tip in my pocket. If I start to have trouble with my line, I pull the Q-tip out and start at the tip of the rod and work my way toward the butt. I run it around the inside of each guide, and if it pulls the cotton on the Q-tip, I know I have a bad guide, and I'll go get it replaced.

A quick note about putting your hooks through the line guides to store them: Don't do it. Ever. This is one of the easiest ways to

When you're using ultralight line, as I suggest, smooth rod guides are a necessity. Silicon carbide guides, like this one, are just the ticket.

nick or scar your line guides, and the only good fix is to replace the guide. Attach your hooks to your reels, on a spot that won't touch the line or scar the reel.

I like rods that aren't so stiff, that aren't broom handles. A parabolic rod is critical. Now, why parabolic instead of fast-taper? A fast-taper rod, which has a whippy tip and a very solid backbone that goes very close to the tip, is not a good rod for the type of fishing we do, especially if it's graphite. You want to use a rod that is parabolic because the bend in the rod is distributed over a larger expanse of the rod, which lets you cast farther.

I like graphite rods, because the rod returns. In other words, it loads up and then it snaps back to its position. So it helps you set the hook, and it helps you cast farther. The rod loads up as you go to cast and literally flings the lure out there.

But all of this is most important when you hook a fish, especially a big fish, because the rod is fighting the fish and not the angler. You'll notice on big game fishing, such as large tuna fishing, the rods they use bend from the tip all the way down to the butt. It's a parabolic arc. If the rod is graphite,

A parabolic rod gives you the maximum bend when you're fighting a fish, and a graphite rod helps you in the fight, as it always wants to snap back to its original, straight position.

it is immediately trying to load up and return to its original position, where fiberglass will just stay bent. The graphite is fighting the fish, it's pulling hard against the fish. And if it's parabolic as well, it's pulling on an arc that applies even more pressure against the fish.

Another problem with fiberglass rods is that every time they bend, little pieces of fiberglass are breaking inside the rod. Eventually enough 'glass breaks, and the rod loses its stiffness. However, it's a gradual process, and one day you'll just notice that your rod is awfully loose, and you won't realize you've been fishing for months with a worn-out rod.

The parabolic, graphite rods, in my opinion, are far superior for the type of fishing I do. They're easier to cast; they cast farther; and they fight the fish for you, which is better than you fighting the fish alone. That's something you want to bear in mind when deciding which rod is right for you.

REELS

The type of of rods and reels that we use in this type of fishing are basically freshwater bass outfits and trout outfits. You have a multiplicity of choices. You can use my favorite, which is baitcasting rods and reels, or you can use closed-face spinning reels, which still allow you to

A Quantum baitcaster— one of my favorite reels.

feel the line and have the advantage of not allowing a backlash, and are the easiest reels to use.

With an open-faced spinning reel you can get line twist and so forth, but the worst part about an open-faced spinning reel, for fishing my method, is that you can't feel the line. The line's not in your hand, and the type of pressure bite I react to, which is moving your shirt just one-quarter inch away from your chest, is so light, so hard to detect sometimes, that you want to be able to feel the line.

Open-faced spinning reels are popular with many people because of their ease of use, but they're a handicap when you're fishing my method, because you don't feel the line as well as you do when you are using a baitcasting reel.

One thing I like on spinning reels is the trigger that allows the bail to be opened with one finger and one hand. I think it's a great feature. Every manufacturer makes one or two models with that feature, and some manufacturers make all of their reels with that feature, because it's handy.

I like a quality fishing reel, whether it be a baitcaster, a spin-caster or a spinning reel. A quality reel handles better. I like power handles, and pads, instead of the round knobs. When I'm fishing my method, my hand's on the handle at all times, so I don't want it to slip when I have to set the hook. Therefore, I like the pad-type handles, and I like a

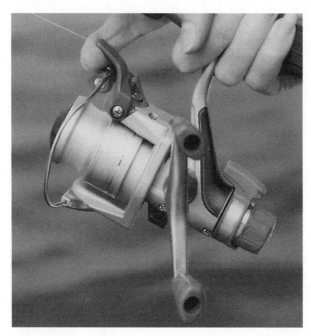

A handy feature on many open-faced spinning reels is a trigger that lets you open the bail with one finger.

power handle that will give me leverage against the fish. Every little edge you give yourself in your equipment will, over time, translate into more fish. Again, it's doing all of the little things right.

Another area of hot debate is retrieve ratios. Do I like the fast retrieves, medium retrieves or slow retrieves? In other words, do I want a reel with six-to-one gears, or five-to-one or four point three-to-one?

For fishing the bays and estuaries, I like fast retrieve reels because I make lots and lots of casts and I don't want to waste time. If I want to go slow, I reel slow. If I want to go fast, I can reel fast and get the line in right away. And the faster I get the line in, the more casts I can make, and the more fish I can catch. So, I like the reels with the higher gear ratios.

Gear ratios are expressed in terms of the number of times the spool turns for each complete crank of the reel handle. So a reel with a six-to-one gear ratio will turn the spool six times every time I crank the handle once, and a reel with a five-to-one gear ratio will turn the spool five times for each full crank of the handle.

Does this make a difference? Sure it does. Without getting too technical on the numbers, a reel with a six-to-one gear ratio gives you a twenty percent increase in line retrieval over a reel with a five-to-one gear ratio, because the six-to-one will get one more spool turn every time the handle is cranked.

If you and I are fishing together, and I'm using a six-to-one reel and you're using a five-to-one reel, and we're both casting the same distances, I'll make six casts for your every five. Over the course of the day, when we're making hundreds of casts, I'm going to make twenty percent more casts than you do. That's going to add up to more fish for me. I'm oversimplifying somewhat here, but I think you get my point.

Of course, you're probably thinking, "If higher gear ratio reels are so great, why do they even make the lower gear ratios?" Simple. For slow people. No, that's not true. If you're fishing for bigger fish, and I mean really big fish, the lower gear ratios give you better cranking leverage than the higher ratios.

Essentially, the trade-off is between speed and power. If you need the power, the lower gear ratios are the way to go. But in the bays, we're getting mostly smaller fish, and will benefit more from the speed. When you do get a big fish on a high ratio reel, you can always add to your power by pumping and reeling, using the rod to provide the leverage the lower ratio reel normally would.

Gear ratios are usually clearly marked right on the reel. The higher the ratio, the faster the retrieve rate. This reel has a 6.2:1 gear ratio.

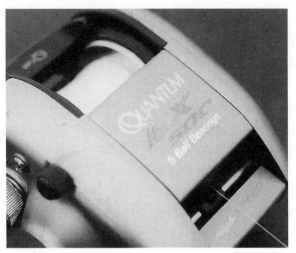

I like reels with a few ball bearings in them, so they're smooth. I make a ton of casts when I'm fishing in a bay, and I want to do it as effortlessly as possible.

I like level wind baitcasting reels because they put the line on the spool. I don't have to worry about laying the line evenly on the spool with my thumb or finger while I'm fighting a fish, which makes my life easier. I've heard some anglers complain that the level wind feature limits the distance of your cast, because the line guide slows down the line on the way out.

Usually, the more ball bearings in a reel, the smoother the reel retrieve. However, as the ball bearing count rises, the price tends to rise as well, so strike a balance you're comfortable with between cost and effectiveness.

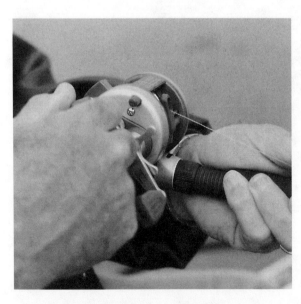

I suppose this could be true, but while I do advocate making long casts in the bay, I don't need mile-long casts, so if the level wind reels do shorten casts, it's not a factor for the way I fish.

The level wind feature takes the headaches (and line cuts) out of putting line back on your spool. It's one less worry you have while landing a fish.

As far as casting with bait-casting reels, yes, a lot of people get backlashes, but they're far easier to use than conventional reels. The most important thing is to practice with it and read the instructions that come with the reel, which explain adjusting the tension knobs on your reel, and whether you have magnets or counterbalance weights to prevent a backlash, which you most likely do. Learn what they're for, and learn how to use them, and you'll be amazed by how easy it is to use these slick little reels.

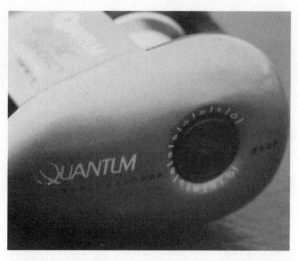

Most baitcasting reels feature some sort of casting control, or magnets that slow down the spool to help prevent backlashes. Read your owner's manual, and use these controls to help you perfect casting with your reel.

The most important backlash control that you can possibly have is your thumb. Just remember one basic tenet: Before the lure hits the water, stop the spool from revolving with your thumb. If you wait until

Casting controls, bells or whistles can never match the effectiveness of a well-trained thumb. It's the best anti-backlash mechanism there is.

after it hits the water, you will have a backlash. Of course, this means that it's particularly important for you to watch your lure all the way to the water, which you should be doing anyway. If, however, you lose sight of your lure during your cast, lose it in the sun or glare or if you get distracted somehow, just go ahead and stop your spool with your

thumb. No, you won't get the great cast you wanted, but you will get a serviceable cast with no backlash, which means you'll be spending your time fishing and not untangling a bird's nest.

Anyway, if *you* get it, it's a backlash; if *I* get it, it's a professional overrun.

Even the best of us get occasional backlashes. Look for the line vee, and use a pick to remove the backlash quickly and easily—well, fairly quickly and easily.

But we all get them and we get them for various reasons. Picking out a backlash can be a trying task. Most people do it incorrectly. All you need to do is look for the vee of line that goes over the line that's going up over the reel. Pull on the vee and your backlash will give way. But pull on everything else or pull on the other line and you will mess it up, or tighten it up, and then you'll usually have to cut out the backlash.

There are little picks made for fisherman to use to pull on the vee in backlashes. They look something like the pick on the end of a pair of nail clippers. You just reach right in there and pull out the little vee, pull up on it, and out it comes. If you fish with a baitcaster, I highly recommend getting one for your tackle box.

Every company makes good and bad reels. They have premium reels and they have inexpensive reels, and with most of the inexpensive reels, you get what you pay for.

I like premium quality reels that are made by Quantum, which is one of my sponsors, but a number of manufacturers make good reels. You do not have to buy the most expensive reel with all the bells and whistles to catch a lot of fish. Bells and whistles catch fishermen, not fish. But if you're the bells and whistles type, go for it. It's your money.

There are a number of equipment tricks that you can use to keep your gear in top shape. When you get a good-quality reel, whether it's baitcasting or spinning, the drag has to be maintained. A number of manufacturers now make a drag grease, which is great. It's not a reel grease. There's a difference between reel grease and drag grease, and you don't want to get them mixed up. You put this on the drag, and the drag will last a long, long time compared to just a short period of time without it.

Usually, when I store my reels, I back off all my drags so the compression on the drag is taken off. The drag lasts much longer this way. You always want to make sure that you have a smooth drag. This is critical. When you're using light, six-pound test line like we are, if you have a jerky drag or a drag that doesn't work well, you're going to break off on every good fish you hook. So you have to have a smooth drag. Drag grease will see to that. Replacing your drag washers periodically will help as well.

LINE

Line, the only link between you and the biggest fish you've ever had on in your life. If you go down to the drugstore and buy a five hundred-yard spool of line for fifty cents, then you deserve to lose the biggest fish you've ever had on in your life. Think of what you spent on your rod. Think of what you spent on your reel, and your tackle and your lures. Do you really want to waste all that money you've invested by cheaping it on your line? Buy a premium-quality fishing line; you'll catch a bunch more fish.

Remember that each fishing line company makes a wide selection of lines for every application. They make lines to flip with; they make lines to troll with; they make lines to fish around rocks and abrasion-resistant lines; they make lines that are extra limp; they make fly lines and floating lines and clear lines; and lines with fluorescence in it so you can watch your line.

Your line is the only connection between you and the fish that just hit your lure. Buy high-quality, clear, abrasion-resistant, monofilament line. I've field tested all kinds of line, and my favorite is Stren Easy Cast.

A basic rule of thumb is use a light, premium, abrasion-resistant line in bays and estuaries. Never use a fluorescent line in saltwater because it spooks the fish. I've found that it cuts down the amount of bites by twenty-fold. So, save your fluorescent lines for freshwater, don't use them for saltwater.

I like to use a balanced line that has good abrasion-resistance, good stretch and high tensile strength. I have found that my very favorite line of all the monofilaments I have ever used is Stren Easy Cast. It's clear, and I like clear lines or white lines, although there are some green lines that seem to work very well in the ocean. I don't like bright blue lines, and I don't like fluorescent line.

There are two real enemies of fishing line: Heat and ultraviolet light. They will deteriorate fishing line. When I fished the first U.S. Open, it was about one hundred twenty-eight degrees on the deck of the boat. By the end of the day, all of the fishing line was rotten. You could take it off in pieces; it came apart in your hand. The heat was so intense that from just laying out in the open, the line had deteriorated.

If you are one of these guys who likes to store your rods and reels in the water heater closet, you are destroying your

Take a look at the line on your reel. How long have you had it? Has it been sitting in the sun? Did you store it in the water heater closet? Is it time you replaced it with fresh line?

line. A little slower, but it's deteriorating. If you're a macho man and you like to put your rods in the gun rack on the pickup truck, it's deteriorating. If you buy any line that has been on display in the window of the store, you're buying faulty line, it's been deteriorating in the sun.

Line gets old. If you store line properly, you can save it for a long, long time. I've used line I've had in the garage for four or five years. But I wrap it in tin foil and keep it in a cool spot, so it lasts a long time. If it dries out, it doesn't mean it's bad. All you have to do is wet it. The white powder that floats to the surface of the line is caused by the line drying out. The molecules of nylon that have floated to the surface of the line are now coming off on your fingers, because the line is dry. All you have to do is get it wet again, and usually it will hold. Pull on it and test it and make sure the line is strong.

Always inspect your line for abrasions. Use good-quality, premium line that is abrasion-resistant. You want a balanced line, a line that has a little stretch in it. Kevlar and microdema lines, such as Fireline or Spectra, have no stretch. That means they're very, very sensitive and they're very good for certain applications. However, if you're using six-pound microdema line, and you get an eight-pound fish and you have a lousy drag, or your reel hiccups, you will lose that fish.

But if you have a monofilament line that has some stretch to it and the fish goes under the boat, the line may stretch and give a little and you have that little extra edge. I don't like the microdema lines for the bays and estuaries because you never know what you're going to hook in a bay or estuary.

You could hook a bunch of little fish, and then the next thing you know catch a world-record fish, like I've done. I caught a forty-two-pound halibut on six-pound test. I've hooked fifty-, sixty-pound fish. I've caught lots of big halibut, lots of big bass. I've caught bass up to nine, ten pounds on six-pound test. You want every bit of edge that you can get to make sure you land that fish. A premium-quality fishing line is the edge that everyone should use. Don't buy cheap line!

You ask a lot of your line. Make sure it's high-quality line that's in good shape, so it doesn't fail you when you need it most.

And change your line frequently. As soon as it starts to show signs of wear, change it. After every cast, I check the first few feet of my line to see whether a fish took it into the rocks or frayed it. You might think it's a hassle to trim up your line and re-tie your lure, but you're going to have to re-tie it anyway after that nice fish you hook next breaks you off because your line was frayed.

Another rule of thumb in bays and estuaries is use a light line, such as four- and six-pound test. The clearer the water, the lighter the line. The difference is astronomical. If you use six-pound test, then go to eight-pound, you'll cut down by twenty to twenty-five percent the number of strikes you get. On ten-pound test, you'll get maybe half as many as I will with six. If you go to twelve or higher, well, enjoy your time on the water.

There will always be some guy that says, "Oh, my goodness, why should I use six-pound test line? I'll lose a fish every now and then." Yes, you will. I don't deny it. Even the best anglers will lose an occasional fish because his line is four- or six-pound test and he hooks into a big fish or his reel gets jammed or his line has a glitch in it and bang, the fish is gone.

So what? You'll get bit again almost immediately. They guy with the heavy test may have to wait hours for a strike. You'll have another strike within a few minutes. Big deal, you'll get another one. You'll have a lot more chances. What do you want, frequency of bite or the rare quality fish? If you want quality fish, if you want to wait for that one big, giant fish, then go ahead and use rope. The problem is you won't get bit as often, and you won't get bit by the big fish as often. I only lose a few of the big fish I hook into. It's up to you—are you fishing, or boating?

It may be difficult to tell the difference between six-pound test (on the left) and twelve-pound test (on the right) with the naked eye, but it makes a huge difference to the fish. You'll get a lot more strikes with lighter line.

I've seen guys catch fish on ten- and twenty-pound test when the bite is wide open. But if the bite gets touchy, I'll outfish them every time. And the bite's touchy a lot more often than it's wide open.

I use the lightest line I can possibly get away with for every kind of fishing I do. If I'm fishing for giant yellowfin, yellowtail or albacore tuna, I use the lightest line I possibly can. For bays and estuaries, even when you troll a crankbait, use six-pound test. Just make sure the drag on your reel is set nice and loose so you don't break off. You don't have to set the hook when you're trolling, the forward motion of the boat will do that for you. So just have your drag set a little loose. You'll just catch more fish with lighter line, period.

There is a proper method of putting line on your reel. On a baitcasting reel, you usually want the line to roll off the top of the spool onto the reel as you wind it on and put a little tension on it, so it's not real loose on the spool. This way when you set the hook it doesn't pull down into folds of the other line. On a spinning reel, you want it to come off the spool backwards, and coil on, so you don't get twisted line. It's important to be careful that you don't get twisted line.

But if you do get twisted line, from either fishing or using a type of lure that twists the line or from putting it on the spool incorrectly, there are two easy methods to rectify the problem. One is, while on dry land, to tie a ball bearing swivel around a tree or to a lamppost. Get your line and just back off, start letting line out and start shaking your line. That will uncoil it.

My favorite solution is to tow it behind the boat. Let out the line off the spool, way more than you're possibly going use that day, and just tow it behind the boat for a short period, just a short distance, without anything on the end of the line, just the line itself, without a lure. That will uncoil the line and straighten it out, and line that you might normally said, "aw, hell, I'll just throw it away," will be fine.

I also want to put in a quick word about tournament, or class, lines versus pound test line. We've been talking all through this book about pound test line, which means that the line will break at a pressure point *not less than* the rating of the line. In other words, six-pound test will hold *at least* six pounds of pressure.

However, if you're interested in qualifying for International Game Fish Association (IGFA) world records, you need to be fishing with tournament or class line, which will break at a pressure point *not more than* the rating of the line. So six-pound tournament line would hold *no more than* six pounds of pressure, and possibly less.

Tournament lines are usually more expensive than pound test lines, so, understandably, the shelves at the tackle shops are dominated by the less

expensive pound test lines. This is not a bad thing, but you need to be aware that if you should ever want to submit a fish for an IGFA record, they will test your line under tournament standards, and there's a very real chance that your pound test will not

If you want to be eligible for world record consideration for your catches, you'll need to be using tournament line, and not pound test.

qualify for the line strength class you submitted it for,

which will push your fish into a more difficult, higher line class. Basically, you may not get your record.

This happens quite often, and is a decision each angler has to make for himself. If you're fortunate enough to land a world class fish, are you going to want to submit it for IGFA consideration, and is that possibility worth the extra cost of the line and the extra times your line will break? It's your call.

LURES

My favorite lure for fishing bays and estuaries is a lead-head jig with a plastic bait on the back of it. There are two types of the plastic lures that I like: the curly tailed grub, a single tail; and the straight tail shad, which is a type of fish body swim bait. That's the one with the knob tail.

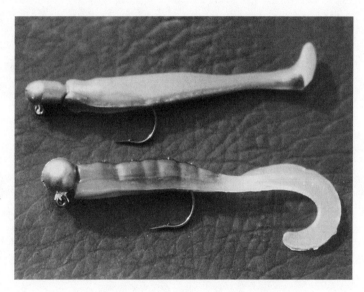

There's a number of good plastics out there. My favorite brand is AA's. Everything I use is made by AA's Lures. It's a hand-poured product. I believe that the softer plastics are best because you get more action, or more vibration, from a softer plastic than you do from a harder plastic. That's why I don't use some of the other lures, because they're made of a much harder plastic. AA's doesn't use any hardener in their plastic, which is why their lures are so soft.

Some guys will say, "Well, harder baits last longer." Well, okay, so you catch two extra fish with it. I'm going to get bit and I'm going to catch way more fish than they are because I'm using the soft plastic bait. I've got better vibration, I've got better strike inducing movement and action. I'll stick with the softer plastic.

Tackle shops love the soft plastic because you only get one or two fish per lure, then you've got to buy more. But you should love it, too, because you'll catch more fish with the soft plastics, and that's the most important thing.

With soft plastic, fish will hold onto it longer because it feels more natural to them. When a fish is sitting around on the bottom of the bay, and he sees your lure come rolling along, he thinks, "Hmm. That looks good," and more likely than not, he'll just flare his gills and displace the water in his mouth, sucking in your lure.

That's that pressure bite I keep talking about. That subtle little pull or tick on your line is your lure hitting the inside of the fish's mouth. Set the hook! But you've only got a second, because that's how long it takes for the fish to realize your lure's not food, and spit it out. The softer bait fools the fish for just that smallest

When fishing my method, you're going to get lots of bites, and catch tons of fish. You'll go through quite a few lures, especially if you use the soft AA's. Always keep plenty of extra lures on hand, so you don't run out of lures before you run out of day.

amount of extra time, giving you one more little edge in catching him. Stick with the soft baits.

Be sure to keep your plastic lures tucked neatly in plastic bags in your tackle box, or things will get a little slippery. When any of these plastic baits or lures sit for any period of time, they'll start to feel oily. The manufacturers don't put an oil on them, it's just the plastisol itself that leaches out and makes it oily. The longer they sit, the more plastisol leaks out. It's no big deal, but it can make your tackle box really messy.

Freshwater plastics will work in the saltwater. The ones I use have been adapted to saltwater by using certain colors, but they're essentially a freshwater bait.

I like to use lead-heads. The biggest, most common mistake I see guys make, is they use the wrong type of lead-heads for the wrong plastic. These lures are designed to produce a specific vibration in the water, which attracts a strike. If you use the wrong lead-head with your lure the vibration changes, and you're negating the whole purpose of the lure. And it will show in your results. I like to use the lightest lead-head that will get me to the bot-

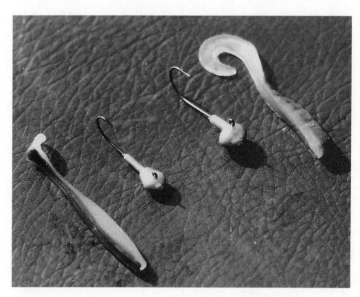

Be sure to select the proper lead-head for the type of lure you're using. The wrong lead-head can give your lure an improper vibration, and make it ineffective.

tom, because I want the lure to roll along the bottom in the current and look as natural as possible.

Fish feel the vibration of anything around them through their lateral lines, which are located on their sides, usually running from their gill to their tail. A bass may be blind and still be able to track a moving object by sensing the object's vibration by using its lateral lines. The type of vibration a lure puts out can trigger a vicious strike or turn the fish off.

I'm sure you've seen times when one lure is working better than another, and that's often because of the different vibrations the two lures produce. It can even be two of the exact same brand, and same type of lure, but one catches more fish than the other. Maybe one's vibrating slightly differently than the other. Sometimes the fish prefer one type of vibration, other times they like a different kind.

Vibration is one of the keys to fishing success. The vibration a lure puts out is what can attract a fish to the lure. Scent is important, color is important, but vibration is the number one consideration for attracting fish. Check your lure when you put it in the water, and if it's not swimming properly, bring it in and fix it. It will make a big difference in the number of strikes you get.

Vibration is what attracts fish to your lure. Make sure your lure is swimming properly before you cast out. Notice how the water ripples differently off the lead-head than it does off the tail.

If you're going to use the shad-type plastic bait, you should use the fish-type narrower head, so the water can go around the lure aerodynamically. The water must pass around the lead-head and move the tail of the long bait and the long tail to produce the proper vibration. That's critical. The pinched or diamond-shaped heads or the fish-type heads that are narrower allow that movement.

With the curly-tailed grub, you can use the football heads, because they don't need water flow to achieve their proper vibration.

I don't like the double tails in the bays because of their larger silhouette. I like the smaller baits in the three inch, either the curly tail grub or the fish bait, the little swim bait, which is called either a swim bait, a knob tail or a shad bait, but they're all the same thing.

The lures are easy to assemble, but it's important that you take care, and do it correctly.

First, insert the hook in the end of the lure, making sure the flat side of the lure faces the lead-head.

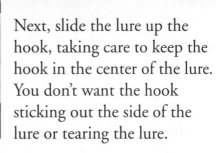

Next, slide the lure up the hook, taking care to keep the hook in the center of the lure. You don't want the hook sticking out the side of the lure or tearing the lure.

When the lure is about even around the curve of the hook, bring it back through the lure, but don't slide it up against the lead-head yet.

Put one drop of Crazy Glue on the plastic lure and then slide it up against the lead-head. That's one drop, not a huge glop. The lure's now ready to use—you don't need to wait until the glue sets up. The glue will set as soon as it hits the water. If you get any on your fingers, just put them in the water, the glue will set, and you won't have to worry about gluing your fingers to your nose, or anywhere else.

It's very important that the lure is straight. If it's crooked, or if there's a hump in the middle of it, it won't produce the proper vibration in the water, and you won't catch fish, or at least as many fish as you would with a properly rigged lure.

If I could only take one lure with me on a bay fishing trip, it would be a AA's curly tail

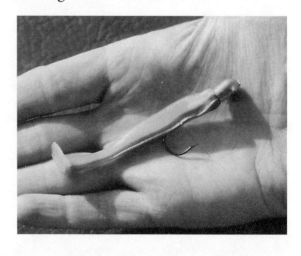

grub, in chartreuse and gold, with a football lead-head. Some other colors work fairly well, clear with red flake, rainbow trout and root beer, to name a few, but over ninety percent of the time you'll find a chartreuse and gold curly tail on the end of my line.

Hard baits, such as crankbaits, deep divers or shallow runners, usually work well for bays and estuaries. One of the things I like to do on my crankbaits is take off the bronzed hooks and put on cadmium-plated or nickel hooks, because they don't rust as quickly. I like fishing with bronzed hooks on my lead-head jigs, because if I do break off in the fish's mouth, the hook rots away rather quickly.

However, on a crankbait that costs ten dollars I don't want one of the hooks to be rotten the next time I go to use it, and I reuse them constantly. With lead-head jigs, you use them, they break off, it's no big deal. But a crankbait you'll use over and over and over again, so I like to use cadmium-plated or nickel-plated hooks.

I don't usually use hard baits to cast out and retrieve like you do fishing in freshwater, where you fish a point, and cast the lure out and retrieve across a point. I never do that with those lures. It doesn't work nearly as well as the plastic baits will. If I'm going to use hard baits in the bays and estuaries, I troll.

Two effective crankbaits for trolling in the bays, harbors and estuaries are the shad deep-diver (top) and the rainbow trout pattern (bottom). Both of these lures are made by Rapala.

CLEANING YOUR GEAR

Everyone knows you need to take care of your tackle, but I often hear anglers ask what are the best ways to do it. First and foremost, you need to clean your gear immediately upon returning from your trip. I do it on the wash rack at the dock, while I'm cleaning up my boat.

If you can't clean it when you get off the water, do it immediately when you get home. Not after dinner, not after you shower, not after you sit down and relax—immediately. Because as soon as you do something else, your gear is as good as forgotten, and even if you do get to it the next day, which is doubtful, the damage has already begun.

A good way to clean your rods is by using a sponge to apply a mixture of a mild liquid detergent and water, being careful to wring most of the liquid out of the sponge before you wipe down the rod. This will remove salt deposits and basic bay muck that you may have picked up during the day.

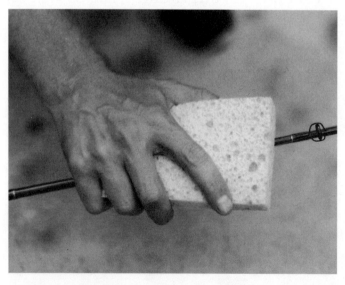

A sponge dipped in a solution of warm water and mild detergent will remove salt deposits from your rods. Be sure to wring most of the moisture out of the sponge, and to rinse all of the soap off your rod.

Use a soft-bristled toothbrush, dipped in the same solution, to clean those hard to reach areas, such as in and around the rod guides. These are the first areas corrosion usually starts, and you want to be sure to give them a thorough cleaning.

Rinse the rods thoroughly with fresh water, and towel them off with a chamois or soft, lintless towel. This will prevent water spotting on your rod's finish.

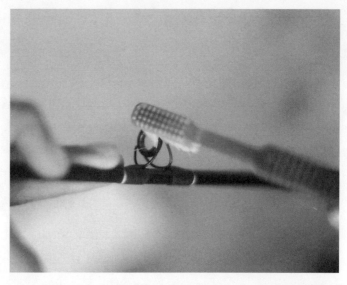

A soft-bristled toothbrush can get to those hard-to-reach spots on your rod where salt deposits like to form. Use the same warm water/mild detergent mixture you used to clean the rest of your rod.

This is also a good time to perform a quick inspection of your rods and guides, to make sure nothing was damaged during your trip. Are the guides cracked, nicked or broken? Are there any cracks in the rod finish, or are any of the wrappings starting to unravel? It's always easier to fix these problems before they disable your equipment, and ruin your next fishing trip.

It's particularly important to clean your reels thoroughly after each trip, because salt will act like sand if it gets into the gears. Wash your reels in the same manner you used on your rods, using a sponge dipped in a mixture of mild liquid detergent and water. Again, be sure to wring any excess liquid from the sponge before wiping down your reel.

Never submerge your reels in a bucket or sink full of water, as it's easy for the water to find its way into the inner compartments of the reel, and begin the corrosion process. The toothbrush you used on your rod guides will come in handy on your reel as well, and be very careful to get everything clean.

Once you've finished washing your reel, rinse it immediately with fresh water, being extra careful to get as little water into the reel as possible. Sort of just pass the water over the reel at an angle, avoiding direct hits right on the reel. You don't want the water to strike the spool directly, as that leads directly to water inside the reel, which gets you corrosion. Spray it lightly, don't drown it.

Set your rinsed reels on a piece of thick terry cloth, and let them drip dry for fifteen minutes or so, then finish the job by toweling them off.

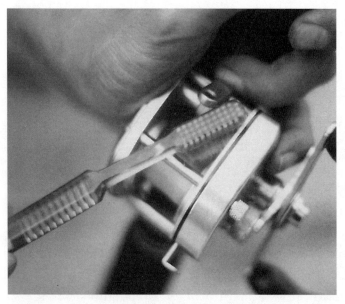

You want to be sure you back off your drags before storing your reels, to prevent the washers, disks and spacers in the drag from freezing together. It also helps to keep some of the flexibility in the disks, which will prolong the life of your drag. But there a couple of different schools of thought as to when to back off your drag.

The toothbrush is also very effective in giving your reel a thorough cleaning. Reels are particularly vulnerable to damage from salt deposits, because of the gears and ball bearings they rely upon to work, but be careful while you're scrubbing that you're not forcing soap into the inside of the reel.

Some people say you should back it off as

soon as you get back, so you won't inadvertently leave it tightened down while the reel is being stored. Others point out that if you back off your drag before you clean your reel, you leave yourself open for getting water into the drag, and they recommend tightening your drag before you clean your reel to keep any water out of the drag, and then loosening it before you store the reel, after it's dry.

I suppose if you can remember to back off the drag last thing before you store your reel, the second way is probably the safer way to go, but it's really up to you.

Before you put your rod and reel away, be sure to take a quick look at the line. Is it frayed, oxidized, chafed or just plain worn-out? Can you remember the last time you changed it? Is there enough line on the spool to do the type of fishing you plan to do next? If not, don't store the reel. If you don't feel like respooling it right then, at least leave it out so you can get to it before you want to head out next. The last thing you want is to be on the water your next time out, take one look at your reel and realize your line's no good. A little foresight can prevent a ruined day of fishing.

Never spray your reel directly with water. Rather, use glancing shots across the reel to rinse it off with as little water as possible. Be sure you've tightened the drag before you rinse the reel, to prevent water from getting inside the drag, but always remember to loosen it again once the reel has dried, to prevent flattening out the drag plate.

THE TRICKS 3OF THE TRADE

One of the best sources of information for new anglers or any angler looking to improve his fishing is the local tackle shop. Ask the guy behind the counter, "What lures are good where I'm going," "Where's a good place to fish," "How deep are the fish?" And don't be shy. Ask any question that you think will help, and don't be too proud to admit you don't understand.

Don't go to K-Mart, where the girl just came out from selling bras in the lingerie department, and say, "Hey, where's the best fishing in Newport Bay and what's the hot lure?" She won't be able to tell you. She's going to say, "34B?"

Your best bet is to go to a dedicated tackle shop or the local pro shop and quiz the guys. They'll tell the truth. They want you to catch fish, so you'll come back and buy more tackle. If you're successful, they're successful, and if you're not successful, they're not successful.

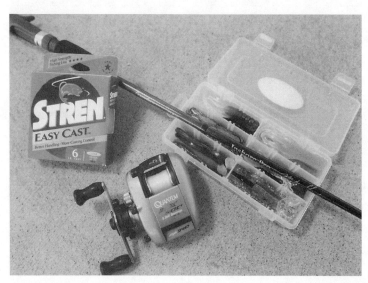

These guys are happy to talk fishing, and can demonstrate equipment for you, show you what's new and what other anglers have been doing, and basically fill in any gaps you may have in your fishing technique. Most tackle shops also offer rod and reel repair service, which you'll really appreciate the first time you've got to ship that reel you bought at a superstore back to the manufacturer for repair.

And if you find the rare tackle shop that's not helpful, or gives you a bunch of attitude, let your fingers do the walking and take your business elsewhere. You want to go to the type of tackle shop that's helpful, and where you feel comfortable. A good, local tackle shop can add quite a few fish to your day's catch, and help keep the number of bad days to a minimum.

And one last thing, please don't grill the guys at your local tackle shop, take all of their advice, drink their coffee and then buy your equipment at the local sporting goods superstore. Yes, the prices may be lower at the superstore, but the information you're getting is worth something too, isn't it? Because if the day comes that the only place left for you to buy your tackle is the superstore, you'll find out just how helpful "34B" is to your fishing.

DULL HOOKS MAKE BIGGER STORIES

How can you tell if your hooks are sharp? "Well," you might say, "if it's a new hook, it must be sharp." You would be wrong. The vast majority of hooks are dull right out of the box, and if you haven't sharpened them, you're fishing with dull hooks and losing fish.

It doesn't take a genius to realize that sharp hooks will penetrate a fish's mouth better than dull hooks, but most people would be surprised to know the difference it will make in your catch count. Again, it's doing all of the little things right that will make you a good angler, and this is one of the little things that's really important.

How many times have you seen people test hooks on their fingertips? "Gosh, feels sharp." It should, since your fingertips are relatively sensitive. But which do you think is closer in toughness to a fish's mouth, your fingertip, or your fingernail? So what should you be using to test the sharpness of your hooks? Your fingernail.

If you can run the point of your hook across your fingernail without it sticking, that is a dull hook. Ladies, this is what you take the men along for when you go fishing, so you don't have to screw up your nails. A sharp hook will stick to your fingernail when you try to run it across; a dull hook will slide. It's that simple.

If your hook is dull, sharpen it. If you don't own a hook sharpener, get one. I prefer the round, diamond hook files with a groove in them over the flat stone type, but whatever works for you is fine. If you've never sharpened your hooks, I can guarantee that nearly every hook in your tackle box is dull. Check them before you use them, and make sure they're sharp.

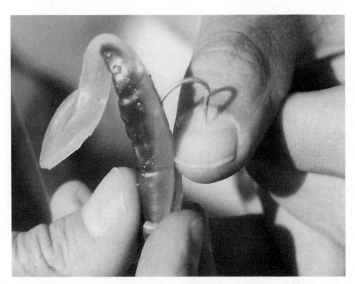

Test the sharpness of your hooks by trying to run them across your fingernail. If they stick, they're sharp. If they don't, they need sharpening.

A number of manufacturers are now selling premium hooks advertised as "sharp," and in most cases they are, and don't need sharpening right out of the box. But it doesn't hurt to check them; just be careful.

Also, dragging your lure across the bottom, scraping it against rocks and pilings and even catching fish doesn't exactly hone your hooks to a razor point, so check your hooks regularly while you're fishing, and sharpen them as necessary. It's the

Keep your hooks sharp and check them regularly. This is an Eze-Lap hook sharpener, which I prefer.

difference between having big fish, and having big stories.

KNOTS

There have been entire books devoted to the single subject of knots. Bad knots are one of the primary reasons people lose fish. It is vital to your fishing success that you can tie good knots, every time. You Boy Scouts out there are probably thinking this is your big chance to use that knowledge you gained getting your merit badge. Sorry, I'm going to keep it real simple.

My favorite knot is the Palomar knot. Why? Because it doesn't cut into itself; it works on line from one-pound test to eighty-pound test. There are, however, better knots than the Palomar on the higher end of the line scale, from fifty pounds on. But we're not using those lines, so I'm not going to deal with those knots.

Knot strength is rated based upon the percentage of the line rating the knot will hold. For instance, to keep the math easy, a ninety percent knot in ten-pound test line will break at nine pounds of pressure

There are knots that are one hundred percent knots, like the nail knot, the Snell knot, the Miller knot, the Crawford knot. These are all really good knots. And they all take a tremendously long time to tie compared to the Palomar knot.

The Palomar knot is extremely easy to tie; anyone can learn to tie it. It's quick, it's easy, it's simple, and it retains about ninety-six to ninety-seven percent of the knot strength. An improved clinch knot, on the other hand, retains only ninety-two percent of the line strength; a uni knot, about ninety-four percent.

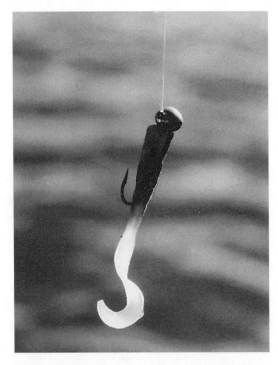

A properly rigged curly tail grub on a football lead-head, tied with a Palomar knot. If you tie the knot correctly, it's one of the simplest and most effective knots you can use.

With the Palomar knot you're sacrificing three to four percent of your line strength, in return for being back in the water much quicker than you would with the higher rated knots. I think it's a fair trade.

The Palomar knot is a good, strong knot, is easy to tie and it will give you the ability to fight the fish without breaking off. If you break off at the knot, you'll have a little hook in the line at the end, and then you'll know you probably screwed up in tying the knot.

To tie the Palomar knot, double about four inches of the line, and pass it through the eye of the hook. It may be easier, especially on smaller hooks, to pass the tag end through the eye of

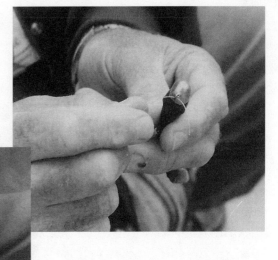

the hook, and then double it back through, forming your four inch loop.

Holding the loop in one hand and the tag end and standing line in the other, tie an overhand knot, being careful not to twist the lines.

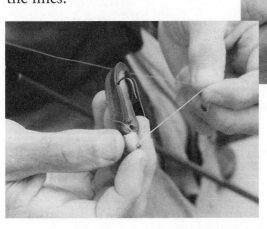

Pass the hook completely through the loop, making sure everything is behind and above the eye of the hook.

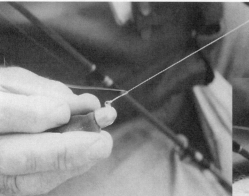

Tighten by pulling only the tag end. You should find that the tag line has curled up somewhat,

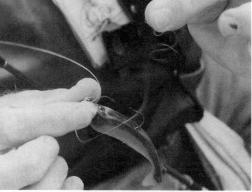

meaning that it absorbed all of the friction and heat, which is what you want. Always draw the knot tight with a steady, continuous pull, rather than jerking it or snapping it tight, as this can weaken the knot. Some people like to moisten their knots with saliva, which reduces the friction and makes it easier to draw up.

Trim the tag down about one-quarter inch from the lure. Be careful not to trim the tag line too close to the lure, as all knots will pull a little before they're fully seated, and you don't want the tag end to pull through the knot when this happens.

Nail clippers are a very handy tool to have in your tackle box. But don't swipe the ones out of the bathroom—buy your own.

If the standing line has curled, you've tied the knot incorrectly, and weakened the line. Cut the lure off above where the line starts to curl, and try again.

When trimming your knots, use a nail-clipper or your dykes, if they're sharp, rather than your knife. It's very difficult for your knife to make a clean cut without stretching the line, whereas the clippers or dykes can snip the line without stress. And for heaven's sake, don't use a cigarette to trim fishing line. Yes, it melts it real nice, and it takes the strength right out of the line at the same time.

Having said all that about the Palomar knot, let me add that it's not a bad idea to learn a number of knots. Did I hear a muffled cheer from the Boy Scouts? Anyway, Stren offers a good fishing knot book, for free. I strongly recommend you write to them and request your copy.

High Tech Gizmos

I will outfish you every time using electronics. Why? What was the number one reason I catch more fish? Quickly. I fish where the fish are.

A good fishfinder will increase the number of fish you catch significantly, because you'll spend much more of your time where the fish are, and much less of your time where the fish aren't.

I am always on the fish because I use my electronics. I still look for all of the other tell-tale signs. I look for where the birds are, I look for the shade. One of the most important basics of fishing is to know your quarry, know where he goes. What turns him on? Why is he where he's at? What is he looking for?

One of the reasons fish are where they are is food sources. Fish want to be where there will always be food nearby. They're sort of lazy that way. But that's actually the number two reason why fish are where they are.

The number one reason fish are where they are is they can find the one thing a fish must have every minute of its life: oxygen.

One factor that affects the oxygen level is the pH of the water. I have a meter on my boat that measures whether the water is too alkaline or base, and where the happy medium is. In some areas with a lot of vegetation and growth, the water becomes a little less oxygenated and has a higher pH. Game fish avoid areas where there's a lot of decaying vegetation, and certain other areas, because of this lack of oxygen, as will the bait fish.

Your number one rule is look for the bait. On your sonar, your electronics, look for the bait and you will find the game fish nearby. If there's bait in the water, it has oxygen, so the game fish can be there, and they will be nearby.

A good fishfinder is basically a sonar just like the Navy uses. It sends down a cone-shaped sound wave from a transducer. It's the little ping that you see in the movies, when the Navy guy is looking at a submarine. That cone of sound goes down to the bottom, bounces off the bottom or anything in between, it turns back up and goes into the machine, which is a miniature computer. The computer decides what it is, whether it's a fish or the bottom and it displays that on the screen as such.

There are different cone angles; many of the popular models use a sixteen degree cone angle. Let's say you have a ten degree cone angle. You have a cone angle that for every degree of angle will show one foot of the bottom in a circle. The cone goes down and gets larger as it goes down. The deeper it goes, the wider the cone. So, if you have a ten degree cone angle, in ten feet, you are looking at one foot of the bottom. So, if a guy is looking at his sonar and says, "Well, there's no fish here." They could be right there a few feet away from the boat. When you are fishing bays and estuaries and you don't see the fish on the meter, it doesn't mean they're not there. Just because you are in ten or fifteen feet of water, you are only looking at a very small portion of water under the stern of the boat, where the transducer is mounted.

I have two sonars on my boat, one in the stern and one in the bow. The one that is on the dashboard has the transducer on the stern and is telling me what's behind the boat. For the one on the bow, the transducer is on the trolling motor, hanging down on the bow of the boat, which is twenty one feet away from the one in the stern. I may be on a ledge and the bow is sitting in six feet of the water and the back of the boat is sitting in twenty. I want to know that.

My electronics not only tell me the depth and what fish are in the area, but whatever else is there as well, such as structure and rocks. The thickness of the line shown as the bottom tells you whether its a hard bottom, a soft bottom or a rocky bottom, and will show up on your unit once you learn how to read it. Instruction books that come with every electronic unit will show you what you are looking at. Learn to use your electronics to find the fish.

This is the sonar unit mounted in the bow of my boat. From my chair I can monitor where the fish are at that end of the boat, what the bottom looks like, and how the fish are moving. I can even follow them with my trolling motor, without ever leaving my chair. Pretty neat, huh?

My particular unit, a Bottom Line Tournament Champion[5], has an option called a fish ID, so instead of displaying a hyperbole representing fish, it will show you the fish. My unit shows three different sizes: small, medium and large. It's either a small fish, a medium fish or a large fish, but the computer cannot determine the actual size of the fish. All it can tell is that at that moment in time, it is looking down and there is a small fish, and there is a bigger fish and an even bigger fish.

Everything is relative. The small fish may be three inches long. The medium fish may be five inches long. And the big fish may be twelve

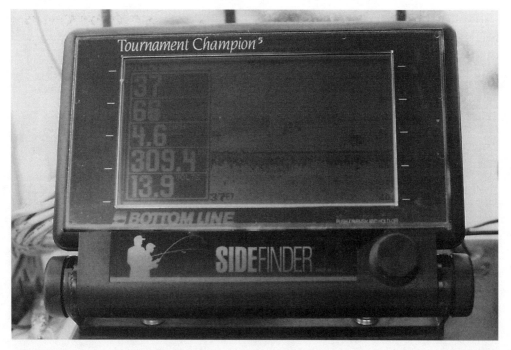

This electronics unit is mounted to the dash of my boat, with the transducer in the stern. We were in thirty seven feet of sixty six-degree water, moving at four point six MPH. We were metering small fish at thirty two and thirty four feet, medium fish at twenty seven feet, and large fish at fifteen, twenty five and twenty eight feet, and there was no bottom structure to speak of.

inches long. Or, you may have a small fish that is fourteen pounds, and twenty five inches long, and the medium fish may be twenty five pounds and thirty three inches long, and you may have a marlin in there that's two hundred pounds. It will show you the same insignia that it shows for the little guys. Small, medium and large. Whatever the computer is seeing at that particular time. If it's swimming and it has nitrogen in its blood or air bladder, the computer picks it up.

It also shows you the bottom and structure. My electronics show me the depth, which is the most important thing to me. Where are we? Are we on the edge of a ledge? Are we on the edge of a dropoff? Is there anything under the boat that is submerged, like rocks and trees, sunken boats, old pier pilings broken up under the surface, pinnacles?

If you learn to understand it, even a flasher, which is the unit with just the little spike on the circular screen, will show you depth and structure. If you can't tell whether that flash is a dropoff or a fish, just stop the boat. If the flash moves, it's a fish, and if it doesn't move, it's a dropoff.

I look for a number of things. Fish, and are they in schools? How deep am I? My unit tells me the temperature of the surface water, it has a little thermometer on the transducer. That's a pretty neat trick. Once you know the habits of the species of fish you are looking for, you'll know whether you are in an area with the temperature that they like.

Different species behave differently as water temperature changes. In warmer water, for example, they'll be more active. If you're in cold water and suddenly the water has gotten very cold, and you find a patch of warm water, that's where you want to fish, because that's where the fish will be.

So electronics are extremely helpful. They show you the structure and structure is one of the keys to success in fishing bays and estuaries. Fish want to hang around structure. I never turn my sonar off. From the minute I launch my boat until I take my boat out of the water, my sonar is on.

Now, why is that? Because I'll be going along and all of sudden I'll come across an island underwater. I'll stop and fish. Or at least stop and meter it to see if there are any fish on it. I've found sunken boats, I've found bodies. There are all kinds of things you can find. Basically, you find fish. If you leave it on and you are constantly looking at it you will also find where the bait is, whether it's down real deep that particular day or if it is up shallow. If they are up shallow, look for feeding game fish down deeper under the bait.

If I'm fishing tight to the shoreline, and my sidefinder spots lots of fish, I know from experience that those are probably spotted bay bass. If I'm out in the middle of the bay or on a ledge, that's probably sand bass. You have to know the habits of the species you're fishing for. They haven't invented a machine yet to tell you what species of fish you're looking at. There are too many species. And besides, I still like to be surprised.

I would never leave the shoreline without a working compass. Anyone who has a boat and doesn't have a compass has at least seven or eight screws loose and their bread is definitely not done.

Anyone who leaves the shoreline in a boat, whether it be freshwater or saltwater, on a big impoundment of water or out on the ocean and doesn't have a VHF radio is totally, absolutely insane and risking their life, and much worse, the lives of their passengers. And nowadays, with cellular phones, take a cellular phone with you, too. You can't be too careful. You should have Vessel Assist now, too, if you're going out on the ocean, because the Coast Guard will not come out and rescue you unless it is totally a matter of life and death. And running out of gas is not a matter of life and death, no matter what you might think.

Electronics are very important on a boat. Always make sure that your radio is functional. That your gas gauge, which is electronic, is functional. Your bilge pump should always work. You may only be out in a bay or harbor, but people have been known to drown in their bathtubs, and the rain doesn't fall and the wind doesn't blow in most people's bathrooms.

PLAYING BY THE RULES

It goes without saying, that anybody over the age of sixteen had better have a license. And if they're fishing in California, they'd better have it displayed between their waist and the tippy top of their head, or they're going to get a ticket. And now, the law has been slightly changed, where the local municipality can add on to any DFG fine that it gets to mitigate in court, so your fines can get pretty stiff.

If you plan on keeping any fish, you need to have some way of measuring them to determine if they're of legal size. Fish rulers, such as these, not only tell you how long your catch is, but what the legal size limit is for a number of different species.

It is your responsibility to know any regulations that govern the area you'll be fishing. Ignorance of the law is no excuse, and you don't want to hear that from a law enforcement officer or game warden.

You must know the size limit and the legal length that you are allowed to keep of each species in your area. You should also be familiar with the species that you catch. You should know the possession limit, the quantity that you are allowed to keep, whether it's five fish, ten fish or whatever.

Sometimes it can get tricky. For instance, in California you currently can catch ten of each type of bass, but you can't exceed a total of ten bass. So if you've got ten spotties, six sandies and four calico, you may not have violated the individual species limits, but you have violated the aggregate limit, which gets you a ticket.

Of course, the easiest way to avoid limit violations is to release what you catch. Again, keep only what you'll eat that night. There's no place in angling for people to kill just for the sake of killing. And if a fish is undersize, throw him back. I don't care if it's halibut, and it's your favorite fish, and you've never caught a keeper and think you never will. Tough. Throw it back. The limits are in place for a reason—species can be depleted a lot faster than you'd think, especially near-shore species.

The Harbor Patrol is there to help and protect you. If you find yourself nervous when they're around, you may want to consider why.

LIVE TO FIGHT ANOTHER DAY

Any time you're fishing, you're exposing yourself to the elements. But if you're fishing from a boat, the effects are often multiplied by the reflection of the sun off the water. You need to be aware of a number of health concerns while fishing, but the one that probably gets the most attention, and yet is the most widely ignored, is exposure to ultraviolet rays.

Any time you are going to be out in the sun, you should be using sunscreen, and a powerful one. Sunscreens are rated in Sun Protection Factors (SPF), which is how much time a person can stay in the sun before he gets burned, compared to how long it would take that person to burn without the sunscreen.

The important part about this is that two people wearing the exact same sunscreen are going to burn at different time intervals, based on their skin types. If you're very fair complected, even the strongest sunscreen won't give you much protection, because you probably burn just looking out the window. And an SPF of one hundred times the fifteen seconds it takes you to burn is no time at all. So wear lots of sunscreen and reapply it often, but keep in mind how long *you* can actually stay in the sun.

A doctor once told me that the sun's rays go right through most clothing. The T-shirts and long-sleeved cotton shirts I thought were protecting me from the sun only gave me about eight to ten percent protection, like a mild sunscreen, and then the rays penetrate. I had been wondering why I was still getting skin cancers, even though I was being very careful to wear my long-sleeved shirts. The doc recommended wearing sunscreen under my clothes.

And you are a fool if you go out without sunglasses. You should always wear polarized sunglasses, which are not only good protection for your eyes, but let you see below the surface, so you can see the fish, the bait, the structure and the weeds where you want to fish.

Use side shields on your glasses if you can. Fisherman's glasses always have side shields to protect you from the sunlight coming in from the side and to protect you from any errant hooks or sinkers that come flying toward your eyes. I had my eye poked right out of my head a number of years ago by a sinker that went into the side of my eye and pushed it right out. Since then, the number one rule on my boat is, "You shall not hook nor hurt the guide." I make everyone repeat that when they first climb aboard.

Naturally, you should wear some sort of a hat. Most fishermen wear a baseball type cap or a billed cap. That may not always be the best way to go for protection, but I have tried all these other caps, with a bill on the sides and on the back and neck protection and everything. The problem is that when you're near-shore casting, you're casting differently than you are if you're casting with iron.

A good pair of polarized sunglasses, such as the Ocean Waves glasses shown here, are a worthwhile investment for any fisherman.

The rod is held near your head and you're constantly hitting your hat if you have a wide brim. A baseball cap is easier. If you really want a good sun protection, you should have a baseball cap that has flaps that come down over your ears and over your neck. You'll look like a dork, but at least you won't have skin cancer. Been there, done that—I've had a number of malignancies removed from my arms. I own the hubcaps on my skin doctor's Mercedes, just because of that.

You also should be careful to avoid exposure problems such as sun stroke, heat stroke and heat prostration. You probably won't get cancer from these, because you probably won't live long enough to get it. You'll just die right there.

When we used to go to Lake Mead or Lake Mohave to fish in bass tournaments, they'd have a doctor speak to us before we started about heat prostration and heat stroke and how easy it is to die from it. Don't let yourself get dehydrated.

Then there's the other side of the exposure coin, hypothermia. If it's going to be cold, dress in layers; it's always easier to peel. You can get chilled out on the water and it may never go away. Never go out on the water, even in the summertime, without a jacket or some type of protection from the elements. What if your boat breaks down and you're stuck overnight? You should have some sort of a jacket or a heavy sweatshirt to protect you from the cold.

It can be the middle of summer, a hundred and ten degrees inland, and it will be sixty-two degrees during the day on the ocean. And at night it can get down to forty degrees on the ocean—it can be very cold. In the wintertime, you can get hypothermia while sitting in the boat, but if you fall in the water, you can really be in trouble.

If you don't know how to swim, wear a personal floatation device at all times when you are on the water. Who cares if someone thinks you're a dork because you're wearing one? If you can't swim, and you're fishing in an open boat, wear one, because the water is dangerous and anything can happen. And if you fall in the water, just remember—that's where Jaws lives.

THE METHOD REVEALED

All right now, if you've been paying close attention, you're probably sitting there with your light-medium action graphite rod, with a good quality baitcasting reel spooled with six-pound test line, preferably Stren Easy Cast, and a AA's curly tail grub tied to a quarter ounce lead-head jig using a Palomar knot, your hook is razor sharp, and you're asking, "Okay. So how do I catch all of these fish?"

Well, now I'm going to tell you, but first, just a little more patience. I keep saying that the secret to success is doing all of the little things right, and the littlest, and most important, is knowing when your lure is in the fish's mouth.

THE FAMOUS QUARTER-INCH STRIKE

Once again, and this time do it with me, grab your shirt between your thumb and your forefinger and move it one-quarter inch away from your body. If you go more than one-quarter inch, you lie about the size of other things too, if you know what I mean. That is a strike. That is what you're looking for with a pressure strike.

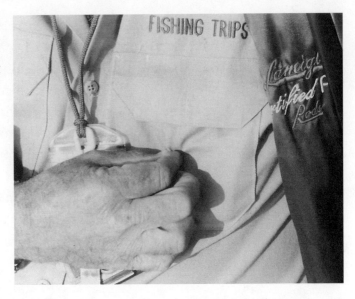

As I mentioned in the discussion about soft baits, the way an in-shore species of fish, usually a bass, strikes a lure is, he flares his gills and literally sucks in the lure. He'll open his gills and create a vacuum, bringing the water through his gills and the lure enters his mouth. He will close his mouth on that lure, and the second he realizes the lure is not real food, that it's not something good to eat, he'll open his mouth and expel it just as quickly as he took it in.

Meanwhile, you're standing in the boat waiting for something to happen. You're waiting for a tap-tap, a tug-tug, a thump-thump, and all you felt was a little tugging of the line. You felt the thumb and the forefinger, pulling the shirt away, right?

That's all you felt. That's a strike. And if you don't react and set the hook, you missed that fish. If you stand up, and you pose for your friends, and say, "Son, I believe I've been bit," and you pose a little more and nothing happens, you missed the fish, because the fish has opened his mouth, spit out your lure and has swum away going, "Man, they bought that lure at K-Mart, and it was two ninety-nine, and I should've known better than to have sucked it in to begin with."

That's what happens when you're unaware that you've just received a pressure strike. If you're chatting with your friends or you're eating your sandwich, there is no way that you will be able to react quickly enough, or even realize that you've been bit.

This is possibly the most important aspect of my fishing method, and it's going to take you a little time to get the feel for it. But it is critical for you to recognize that the lure is in the fish's mouth. I'll say it again: *Fish have no hands!*

Now, you might be thinking, "They hit my live bait awfully hard." Yes, they do. But we're fishing with artificial lures, and the fish take the lures differently, and more frequently, than live bait, because they see the lure

as an easy meal. Chasing live bait requires fast action on the part of the fish. Sucking up your lure while it rolls along the bottom, on the other hand, is much more like home delivery.

One of the biggest reasons I prefer baitcasting reels to spinning reels is that they allow you to feel the pressure strike better—that little tension in the line that means I've got a fish on. Very few anglers are accomplished enough to feel that strike with a spinning rod like you would if you had a baitcaster.

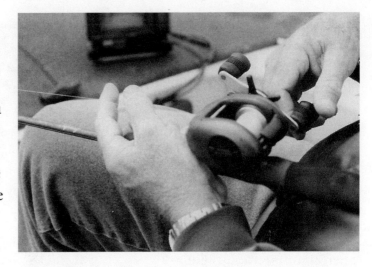

You'll want to remember that if you set the hook, and it's a fish, this fish could be the biggest fish that you've ever had on in your life. You may not have been sure it was anything, it was a little tick. It felt like it bounced on the bottom. Well, the bottom is sand, it doesn't make a tick. But it could be the biggest fish you ever had in your life. It could also be a mermaid, it could also be a submarine, whatever. Set the hook! They're all fun to catch. If anything doesn't feel normal, if anything doesn't seem right, set the hook.

The strike can be anything. The strike can feel like anything. It's the most important thing to remember. If the lure stops while you're retrieving it, you either have a snag or a fish. You really won't know if you hesitate. If it's a fish, it will spit out the hook as soon as he feels the resistance.

Remember that quarter inch with the shirt—that doesn't feel like anything. The line may get suddenly tight; you have a fish on the other end. The line may jump; you have a fish on the other end, but you don't feel anything. Swings are free. Fish have no hands. They do not have the lure in their hands, tugging on the line. If you're waiting for a tap-tap; a thunk-thunk; a jerk-jerk, or some sort of a pronounced feeling, you're going to miss ninety-nine percent of your strikes.

If you'll notice, I use the word strike and not bite. A strike is when a fish attacks or strikes a lure for any of a multiplicity of reasons. He's angry. He's protecting himself; he thinks it's going to hurt him so he attacks it. He's angry because you invaded his space. He thinks it's food. He is competing against another fish. I'm sure once upon a time you've caught a fish while another fish was trying to take it away from him. There's competition there.

Maybe you just drug the lure through his bedroom. He's spawning and you drug the lure right through his bedroom. If you're spawning and someone drove a tractor trailer through your bedroom, you'd be angry, too, right? And you would be on the attack. Think about that the next time you're spawning.

A bite, on the other hand, is when a fish eats. You've all experienced the most wide open bite, when a fish is going through a school of anchovy with its mouth wide open and feeding voraciously. You could throw a potato in and the fish would bite. He'll hit anything that's moving that looks like it's food. That's called a positive feeding mode.

There is also a neutral feeding mode. He's sitting by a bush, by a boat dock, by a tree, by a piling. You toss the lure out and he says, "Uh, it looks like it's good to eat. It's no big deal. I'll just open my mouth as it drifts by and pick it off." That's a neutral feeding mode. He can take it or leave it.

A negative feeding mode, when a fish doesn't bite, is when he's full, when the moon says that he shouldn't eat or the tides are not moving, and for whatever of a multitude of reasons, he's not going to eat anything. Nothing. You could drop a live bait in front of him, you could drop every artificial lure in your tackle box, he won't hit it. That is a negative feeding mode. There is only one lure that works at that time, and that's called a green and yellow hand grenade. Blow his butt out of the water, and he's yours. Other than that, it's not going to work (and I was just kidding about the grenade). That's a negative feeding mode.

But even in a negative feeding mode, a fish will strike a lure for other reasons. You have your trusty curly tail grub. He's guarding that piling. That's his piling. He's in there and he's got his eye right in the shady part of that piling, so he feels safe and secure. You throw that curly tail right by his face five times and he ignores it. He says, "I'm not going to let it bother me." Then you throw it again, and he says, "Now, if you do that one more time, I'm gonna tear you up." Then you do it one more time, and he hits it. You just became a fisherman using a reaction bait, which forced a reaction from the fish. You got him to take the lure, that's a strike, not a bite.

CASTING

I always tell people I want them to make long casts in bays, estuaries and harbors. The majority of these are shallow—anywhere from extremely shallow, inches of water, down to sixty feet, seventy feet. You usually won't find any of the near-shore areas that you'll be fishing to be any deeper than that. Therefore, the predominant depth of what you fish in bays and estuaries and harbors is usually between zero and twenty-five feet. You have to make a long cast. You are fishing six-pound test line that sinks rather rapidly, because there is less water resistance on lighter line.

You are fishing with light lures. A quarter-ounce lure, quarter-ounce lead-head jig with a plastic grub is going to sink possibly as fast as one foot per second. You always want to use the lightest lead-head you can that will get you to the bottom. It will eventually get to the bottom. Sometimes you want it to get there right now, sometimes you want it to go slower. You have to ascertain which it is by trial and error.

Therefore, if you know, because your depth finder shows you, that you are in fifteen feet of water, your lure goes down ten feet and stops sinking, you don't feel anything, but your line jumps, set the hook. If you feel anything, your line doesn't move, your line stops moving, set the hook.

Making long casts, up-current, will increase your chances of catching fish with each cast.

You're in the top of a tree, you're in a submerged boat, you're in a number of different things, but you may also be in a fish's mouth. He has flared his gills and sucked the lure in, and he's holding it in his mouth for that millisecond before he realizes that it isn't real. That's why people use phony scents on their lures, so that fish will hold that lure one millisecond longer than he normally would. Personally, I don't think scents are worth the effort most of the time, but it can add just a little to your edge.

But always make long casts, and the best thing to do is to cast up current. Why cast up current? Because the fish are looking up current, waiting for an easy meal to come rolling along as the tide comes in or out. When the current is moving, the fish are facing whichever direction it's moving in, because the current is bringing food to them. Is the water going out of the estuary or bay, back to the ocean, or is it coming in, bringing along crabs, little bait fish, and other fish delectables, with it?

The fish are looking into the current, searching for sand crabs or whatever comes along that looks tasty, and they're going to grab it. If they're in a positive, or maybe a neutral, feeding mode.

Okay. So you're casting up current. It's rolling along the bottom, the fish is looking for an easy meal. If it stops rolling along, set the hook.

Now, current and fast moving water usually mean feeding fish. However, there are times when the current is moving so fast, that you have to slow your lure down to make it look like an easy meal. You don't want it to go by the fish so fast that he doesn't know what to do. For those times, you'll want to use a slightly heavier weight, and give the fish a better chance to strike. You want your lure to tumble along the bottom with the current, so don't go too heavy.

When you cast, immediately engage your reel when your lure hits the water. You may get a strike on the sink, and if your reel's not set, you'll have a backlash when you go to set the hook. Let your lure drop all the way to the bottom, keeping a tight line. Once you reach the bottom, turn the reel handle two or three turns, and let the lure go back to the bottom. Always keep a tight line, so you can feel the fish when he takes your lure.

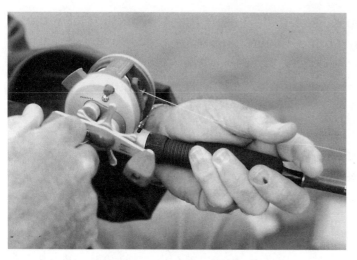

Slowly bring the lure back to you in this manner, turning the reel handle a few times, and letting the lure sink back to the bottom. If you feel anything that doesn't feel right, set the hook! It doesn't have to be a tap-tap, a tug-tug or a thump-thump; sometimes the line

If you feel anything at all through your line—set the hook! Swings are free.

just jumps, or gets a little tighter—that's a fish, set the hook!

Sometimes you'll want to vary this approach a little. Maybe you're going along a deep piling, but you know you can't cast past the piling. You want the lure to sink adjacent to the piling. You think there are calico suspended along that piling, which is something calicos like to do.

What you want to do is cast out toward the piling, and once the lure hits the water, so that there's drag against it, feather the reel or the spool and raise the rod tip to let excess line out to avoid a backlash. Keep the rod tip high, and as the lure sinks, lower your rod so that the lure sinks parallel to the piling or wall. Try to control it.

As the rod tip approaches the water if you still need more line, take your thumb off the spool and again raise your rod tip. But always have your thumb in control of the line, so if you do get bit on the way down, you can immediately turn the reel handle and engage the reel, avoiding a big backlash when you set the hook.

Water temperature controls what a fish does. If the water is cold, he'll be less active. If he's just come out of deep water, it will take him fifteen to twenty minutes for his body to become acclimated and take on the temperature of the surrounding water, and he'll be a little sluggish.

If the fish dives into non-oxygenated water, his body reacts immediately and he comes back into oxygenated water. Same thing goes for uncomfortable temperatures. If he goes into an area where he would be totally uncomfortable, and he has a comfort zone around him where he'd be more comfortable. He's going to spend his time where he's comfortable.

The factors that prevail on a fish's comfort zone are light penetration, water temperature and that one all important thing, other than oxygen, the availability of food. Wherever there is food, a game fish will be nearby. They're not going to let their meals get too far away from them. They have to eat every single day, and they will.

You want to make sure that you vary your reel retrieve. Try it fast, try it slow, until you figure out what speed the fish want the lure to go at that moment in the day.

This speed changes from one moment to the next. They can want it real fast in midday, but in the morning with low light conditions, they may want it to move slow, or maybe vice versa.

Some fish like a fast retrieve, some a slow. This little sand bass hit on a slow retrieve.

These are things that will keep you on your toes and learning. This is called establishing a pattern. Determining where the fish are, what they're eating, how deep they are. That's all establishing a pattern.

Be sure to keep your lure on the bottom. These fish are either bottom feeders or they will be on or near the bottom. They will go down to the bottom to pick something up off the bottom if it looks good to eat. Most of the time, fish can see extremely well in their environment. Far better than you or I can. Make sure your lure sinks all the way to the bottom, and keep it there.

Now, if you set your rod down, and your lure is in the water, chances are that is when you are going to get bit, and that always seems to be when you don't get the subtle pressure bite. You get the WHAM!, and the fish will take the lure in its mouth hard and take your rod over the side. If you need to set your rod down and don't have time to reel in your lure, always put it in a holder. Fate has a twisted sense of humor.

WHEN IN DOUBT, SET THE HOOK!

You must set the hook instantly. When you feel a fish, it will only hold the lure for that little millisecond. He is not going to sit there and munch on it like it's a popsicle. He's going to say this is wrong, this isn't real and spit it out, and you've lost him.

Now when you do get bit, the best way to set the hook when you feel the fish is to raise the tip of the rod upward in a fast motion and *reel at the same time*. This is critical. I know I'm asking fishermen to do two things at the same time, which is really difficult for most fishermen. Swing the rod and reel in line at the same time. If you don't, you'll never get enough pressure on that hook to penetrate the fish's mouth. Most hooks don't penetrate the fish's mouth just by swinging.

When I give seminars, I usually pick out one of the big guys in the crowd, and I wrap my line around his finger and I back off as far as I can, usually twenty-five to fifty feet, and set the hook as hard as I can. Big swing. The crowd usually expects to see the

When you set the hook, swing AND reel at the same time. It makes a heck of a difference.

guy's finger wriggling around on the ground, but the guy can barely feel it, because of the give in the line and the distance between us. He usually feels about one and a half pounds of pressure at his end of the line, at the most.

The fish usually sets the hook itself. It puts its head down and starts fighting, and the rod's got tension on it, which imbeds the hook in the fish's mouth. That's why sharp hooks are so important.

This is also one of the best reasons there is to use a graphite rod. To feel the strike, number one, and number two, so the fish is fighting the rod the whole time. With a parabolic action rod, as the fish pulls on the line and on the rod, the rod is keeping a constant tension on the hook, which is hopefully embedded in the fish's mouth.

If you give a fish slack line, he will immediately throw the hook. Usually, he will wear the hole where the hook is embedded larger and larger as he fights. As he gets nearer the boat the hole has gotten bigger and bigger unless it is in a hard, hard part of his mouth. In that case, if you give

him loose line or if he leaps in the air and gets loose line or slack line, he will throw the hook because of the lead that is attached to the hook. In other words, the lead-head jig will give the fish leverage and he just flips it and goes free.

As a fish tries to fight a graphite rod, the rod is constantly pulling against him, trying to return to a straight position. This makes it easier to keep your line taut.

There are incorrect ways to set the hook. One is the sideways swing, especially if you are in a swivel seat. The seat will do exactly as it was designed to do and swivel, like in a bass boat or in my boat. You

swing sideways and there's nothing there. You'll keep spinning, and you'll spin right off into the water. That's no fun. Been there, done that.

Here's a graphic example of the importance of keeping a tight line when landing a fish. Notice the hole in the fish's lip that the lure has worn through. If he had been given any slack line at all, he would have thrown the hook instantly, and we would have had one less white sea bass that day. Always keep a tight line!

One of the worst things you can do when you set the hook, especially for guys with spinning rods, is instead of keeping the butt low and bringing the forward part of the the rod upward, you raise both arms above your head. This is the worst way you can possibly set a hook. The fish has you, you don't have the fish. You have no leverage.

Who is this guy? This is a perfect example of exactly how NOT to set the hook. You have no leverage whatsoever, and not only are you not going to catch the fish, he's probably going to laugh at you as well.

Both spinning rods and baitcasters have foregrips. The foregrip on the baitcasting rod, or freshwater bass rod, is there for a reason. When you set the hook, you have leverage, you're holding the rod by the foregrip with your left hand, you're holding the reel handle with your right hand, and the rod butt is against your chest. When you swing in an upward motion, you have leverage on the fish.

If you're a macho man, and you're holding the rod by the reel with your left hand, like some of the bass pros do, then the fulcrum or balance of the rod is now disproportionate to the angler. The fish can pull the rod and you have no leverage. Hold the rod correctly.

Always have your hand on the handle of the reel. If you have to try to find the reel handle after you've been bit, that momentary pause while you reach over and grab the reel handle is the difference between hooking the fish and the fish going, "Oh, this isn't real, ptooie," and spitting it out. And you just lost another fish.

REELING HIM IN

There are a couple schools of thought on reeling in the fish. When you set the hook initially, does the hook go in, does it penetrate? Not always. Sometimes it does, sometimes it doesn't. Some fishermen will say they like to set the hook two or three times. I can't find anything wrong with that, other than the fact that it sometimes breaks off, and sometimes they pull it out of the fish's mouth, especially if it's a halibut. They just keep jerking on it, and it pulls his lip off. Your lure comes back and here's a piece of lip on it.

If you want to play the fish, it is critical that you have the right drag set on your reel, whether it's a spinning reel or a baitcasting reel. You must have a smooth drag. When you're selecting a reel to buy at the store, find one that has a real smooth drag right out of the box.

You can also take your reels to your local tackle shop, which is hopefully where you bought them, and say, "Hey, make this as smooth as glass." They can do that. If they can't you might want to do a little shopping for a new tackle shop.

Most tackle shops use the same thing that I do, drag grease. Now, I'm not talking about reel grease, that you would grease the gears in your reel with. I'm talking about a special grease that goes right on the drag washer and will make that drag smooth. A smooth drag is critical when you're fishing on six-pound test line. You never know when you're going to hook a really big fish, forty, fifty, sixty pounds. They can be hooked easily and readily on really light line.

Now, you've hooked him, you've enticed him into striking the lure, you've set the hook and you've got him. Now, what are you going to do? You've got to reel him in. If you've got a bad drag and the fish surges the other way, and the drag catches, with six-pound test, bang, he's gone. Now, monofilament fishing line has a certain amount of stretch in it, so there's a certain amount of forgiveness in it, but only so much. Bad drag, no fish.

A good rule of thumb for me is if I have six-pound test line, I set the drag at approximately four pounds. In other words, it should pull off the reel relatively smoothly, but have enough tension on it. When you pull on it, it shouldn't break. The fish is going to pull on it completely different than you are. A lot of times people will set the drag with the line tied considerably far from the rod tip. I just pull the line straight from the reel, because I've developed a feel over the years.

If you're not comfortable setting your drag by feel, there are special scales made to tell you just how much pressure your drag is set at. Get a scale, tie your lure to the scale, have someone back off from the scale and pull to see what the pressure reads on the scale.

You should never go to the rating of the line, to six pounds for six-pound test, for instance. At that point you've defeated the whole purpose of the drag. The drag is there to allow the fish to take line before the

Your drag should be nice and smooth. If you feel any catches in your drag, or if the line doesn't come off as smoothly as you'd like, take it in and get it serviced.

line breaks, but if you set your drag too tightly, too close to the rating of your line, you've eliminated your margin of error, or at least slimmed it way down.

For six-pound test, I like to set my drag at four pounds. When I troll, I use about three pounds of drag. I don't want to break off. When the fish grabs it, the boat has forward motion and the fish will set the hook himself. The combination of the fish and the boat puts a lot of stress on the line.

When in doubt, I lean toward too little drag rather than too much. I'd rather have too little pressure on the fish, in other words, a smaller amount of drag, than have to to worry about the fish making a sudden surge and having it break.

Always have a good drag, and remember that you don't have to horse him in if it's a big fish. Use some skill, and fight him to the boat. If it's a small fish, reel him in, get it over with. Most people enjoy playing the fish out, but there is such a thing as overplaying the fish.

I strongly support practicing catch and release. But if you play the fish for half an hour, he's totally exhausted. The fish will burn up all his oxygen, and then regurgitate as a last-gasp effort. Once he's regurgitated, if you continue to play him you could actually kill him. He'll have to be revived. Many a time you'll get a fish in that you'll have to hold by the lower jaw and run him through the water to oxygenate the gills, or he's going to die. If you just flip him over your shoulder and into the water, he will die, and that's not really catch and release, is it?

After I set the hook, I always keep a steady pressure on the fish. Sometimes I'll do it twice, by raising the rod. But I keep a steady pressure on him, so as he pulls me down after the initial set, and as he lowers his head and starts to go down, I'll reel down to him and come up again.

Sometimes I just pop my wrist, but I don't slam it home like I do the first time. I never ever give the fish slack line. I always keep a taut line. I keep real steady pressure. But otherwise, you can stop reeling when he pulls you down. Never back off, never stop reeling and give him slack line.

If it's a big fish, the best way to do it is to pull up on your rod, on the rod tip and

Many fish, especially spotted bay bass, will fight you right to the boat, and then some. Be careful about burning up all of a fish's oxygen when you're fighting him. Run his gills through the water a few times before letting him go. Of course, if he's trying to take your thumb off and is flopping you in the face with his tail when he gets to the boat, he probably doesn't need reviving.

not reel. Then after you get your rod in an upright position at about eleven o'clock or eleven thirty, slowly reel, keeping a taut line as you lower the rod. That's how you pull a big fish in.

Another way is if you're out on the open ocean, is to use the swell or the action of the water to help you land a big fish. Guys that have a tuna on and so forth, as the boat comes up they pull on the rod, but don't reel. As the boat comes down, they reel like crazy, keeping a taut line, letting the ocean do the work for them. That way, all they have to do is hold onto the rod as the boat comes up. There's no strength involved, and you don't get worn out. You let the ocean work for you. Obviously, this doesn't factor in much in bays and estuaries, so it's just a bonus tip.

LANDING THE FISH

When you've got the fish to the boat, especially if it's a big fish, you want to put your reel in free spool, but keep your thumb on it to prevent the line from running out. That way, if there's a sudden jerk from the fish, you can release line quickly, rather than let him snap you off.

When I'm landing a fish, a lot of the time on the smaller fish I'll let his forward momentum and the rod absorb the pressure of lifting him out of the water. When he's about two and one-half feet away from the rod tip, I just raise the rod and lift him into the boat. Never grab a graphite rod by the middle—it will snap. And don't reel the fish too close to the rod tip—that's another easy way to snap your nice graphite rod.

Graphite rods are not designed to bend more than ninety degrees. It's a parabolic rod, just let the rod absorb the weight of the fish and the upward action and swing him up and set him down.

When you've got the fish to the side of the boat, be sure to put your reel in free spool, just in case. Of course, this isn't such a hot idea for spinning reels.

Most fish are lost right at the boat. As the fish approaches the boat, if he's too big to bounce, use a net. Don't reach over the side and grab the lead-head jig; that results in many a hook embedded in your thumb or finger. If you slide your hand down the line to grab the lead-head and the fish pulls it out of his mouth and there's an arc in the rod, you will, guaranteed, embed that hook in your finger. This is the voice of experience, and I can tell you, it's not a pleasant feeling.

A lot of the time I will reach over for my customers, I'll look down and see if the fish is well hooked, and if it doesn't look like I'll hurt myself, then I'll reach down and grab the lead-head and swing the fish over. But if he looks like he may just be barely hooked on his lip, or he's not securely hooked, I'll always call for the net. I'll net the fish or one of the passengers who's not hooked up will net the fish.

Kids, don't try this at home. Pulling in fish, especially big fish, by the lead-head is a good way to see how far you can embed a hook into your finger.

California DFG regulations pretty much require you to carry a net if you're fishing in the ocean, but you should have one anyway, regardless of where you're fishing. It's nearly impossible to land a big fish without one, unless you use a gaff, and the gaff doesn't work particularly well with catch and release.

So many fish are lost at the boat because someone screws up with the net, and the person who causes the fish to be lost is often not the angler, which can really strain the mood of a fishing trip. You don't want to be the guy who loses your friend's fish because you cut his line with the net, or tangled the net because you had it in the water too long, or you spooked the fish by going after him too early.

For some weird reason, a big round metal thing coming out of "the other world" really seems to bother most fish. I have no idea why, but it does. So, if you're netting a fish, the fish should be showing some signs of being tired, or he's going to freak out as soon as you go after him with the net.

It's very easy to lose fish with a net. Make sure the fish is starting to show signs of tiring before you net him, especially when it's a big fish.

Always net the fish head first. The angler should use the rod tip to keep the fish's head up, and direct him toward where the net is coming from.

Fish can only swim in one direction, so make that direction be into the net.

When the fish is in position, headed toward the net and tired, quickly scoop the net under his head and bring him into the boat. Do not stand with the net over the side, admiring the catch. This is the best way to find out about that

When the big moment comes, net the fish quickly, smoothly and head first. Remember, they can only swim in one direction...

weak spot in your netting, and how easily a fish can break through it.

As I mentioned earlier, you should also carry a fine meshed net for landing halibut, particularly undersized halibut, which you can mortally injure by netting them with the wrong net.

When it comes time to remove your hook from that freshly landed fish, always remind yourself—fish have teeth, particularly spotted bay bass. I have a number of spottie teeth embedded permanently in my flesh. Calico bass have teeth, sand bass have teeth, but nothing like spotted bay bass. Spotted bay bass have very powerful jaws, and they can and will clamp down on you. Sometimes I think they enjoy it.

I like to reach over the teeth, pinch the flesh of the fish between my thumb and forefinger. Then, I take my other hand, and I grasp the hook. Usually downward pressure, pushing

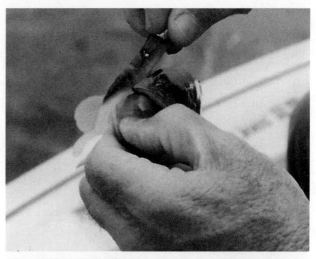

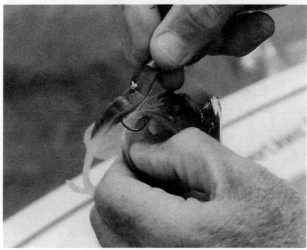

Try to remove your hooks as quickly as possible, doing as little damage to the fish as you can. Never handle a fish with dry hands.

through the same hole that it came in, will work. Sometimes you push down and twist. Other times you must use long-nosed pliers, if it's extremely well hooked.

Do not grasp the fish with dry hands or a dry rag. You take the slime off the fish, and it's like removing your epidermal layer. Wet your hands, or wet a rag, if you have to use a rag on a really slimy fish.

A lot of fish, like the spotted bay bass, if you grasp it by its stomach, but don't squeeze too hard, it will stop moving. And don't stick your fingers in a halibut's mouth or a barracuda's with razor sharp teeth, especially if you have an attachment to that thumb. What I like to do with a fish like that is reach in under his gills, but not damage his gills. I'll take the lure out pulling that way.

Try not to hurt the fish. Sometimes, a fish will bleed, and usually it's not a big deal, sort of like cutting your finger. He'll heal. Maybe a few filaments in his gill are damaged. He'll bleed, but he'll heal. Don't think that just because a fish is bleeding that he's automatically going to die, and kill him or mistreat him. Most of the time a fish is cut in his mouth, or where you've hooked him, and he'll recover, so throw him back and give him the chance to get better.

Many fish will be subdued if you hold them gently by the stomach, but don't get complacent and forget about their teeth and spines.

Now, if you take the arch of the gill and you rip it or tear it, the fish will die. That's like cutting a major artery. It's like ripping out a lung with an artery attached. You don't want to do that, and be careful when handling your fish.

Also be careful, when removing your hook, to keep only enough pressure on the line to help you remove the lure. Too much line tension can release the lure with a snap, and propel it right at you or someone else in the boat. Do not try to subdue a fish by stepping on him, even if you plan to keep him. This is a good way to get stuck in the foot by a spine or hook, and also to have the hook come flying out like I just mentioned.

Be careful to reach over the teeth when handling fish, especially spotted bay bass. If you forget, they're sure to remind you.

Fortunately, fish aren't smart enough to remember the dangers of striking a lure.

Maintaining Your Lures

When fishing with artificial lures, maintaining that lure is extremely important. I fish two different types of lures. I fish with a curly-tailed, which undulates in the water, and I fish with a shad bait, which imitates an elongated fish and has a little knob on the tail.

As long as the lure is intact and has not lost any of its tail, you can use it. The lure can be shredded with teeth marks, and as long as it will stay on the lead-head and the tail still gives a vibration that will entice the fish, it's fine. You don't have to throw it away just because it has a little tear in it. If it affects the action of the lure, then yes, throw it away. But if it doesn't affect the action of the lure, if you can still get the wobble, shake or undulation you're looking for out of the lure, keep using it. A lot of the time, I'll repair it with a little Crazy Glue.

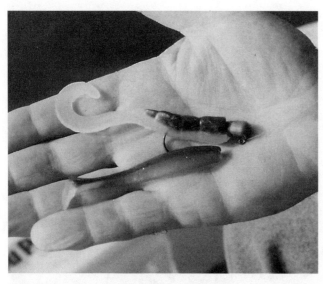

The most important part about maintaining your lures is preserving their vibration patterns. As long as the tails are intact, the lures will work fine, so don't sweat a few teeth marks.

Ah, the secret of Crazy Glue. Crazy Glue is one of the neatest things that's been invented for fishermen who use artificial plastic lures. These have a tendency, even when you use a barb on your lead-head jig, to come off or slide down from the head of the lead-head. The best thing to do is put your lure on the hook and slide it up to the lead-head. Then back it off a bit, and put one little drop of Crazy Glue on the end of the jig, remembering not to put your fingers together if you got glue on your fingers. If you did, stick your hand in the water and the Crazy Glue will set immediately, as it will on the lure. You do not have to wait for it to dry. Put a little drop on the lead-head jig, push your plastic lure up against it over the drop. You can immediately start fishing because as soon as your lure hits the water, it sets it off. Everything is tickety-boo.

Crazy Glue is inexpensive. And it's a whole lot cheaper to buy a few tubes of Crazy Glue than it is to buy a whole bunch of lures, and your lures will last much much longer if you use Crazy Glue.

Never, ever throw your lure back in the water with grass or weeds or some sort of aquatic vegetation or pieces of paper or plastic that have

There's no point in casting your lure if there's vegetation or other debris on it; no fish will give it a second look.

been stuck to it. Always keep your lure clean, because it's the vibration that attracts the fish to it. As he gets closer, he'll look at the color, or the size, and a number of other factors.

But when he first feels the vibration in the water of that lure, that's what attracts him, the vibration. That's what will help trigger a strike. If something is on that lure that will affect the vibration, then why bother to throw your lure? If you put a piece of squid on it that enhances the flavor or the catchability, make sure that piece of squid is not so large that it affects the action of the lure. You don't want anything on that lead-head that will affect the action of the lure.

TROLLING

There are times when trolling is so deadly that you can't get a hundred yards without hooking a fish. For most of what I do, I use plastics, but there are times when trolling can be best.

You can pretty much catch anything trolling. You'll catch bass; you'll catch halibut; you'll catch just about any type of fish. Newport Bay has literally been raped by anglers trolling. I taught these guys how to do it and I taught them what lures to use. Nobody ever used to troll in Newport, and the fish were always there, but these days it's kind of slim pickings.

My method is extremely effective whether you're in the harbors, bays and estuaries or out, and you'll usually catch more fish than you will trolling. Trolling is great for the days when the action just isn't happening, and you can cover a large amount of water in a fairly short time.

But for most days, I can catch four or five fish casting in one spot in the time it takes you to shut off your motor, land the fish, release him, get your lure back in the water and get it out behind the boat.

When I troll, I don't just drag the lure around the bay behind the boat. I think that's boring, and it leaves a little too much to chance. I never put my rod in my rod holder. I hold it in my hand, so I can work the lure while I'm trolling.

There are a number of crankbaits that work well for trolling. Most of the time you'll find that the chartreuse colors, in the dirtier water, work well, and the chromes and brighter colors work better in the clearer water. I like chromes with black backs, I like chromes with blues and I like tiger stripes. Chartreuse shows up in muddy water really well. You'll find that stick baits, the jointed and broken back minnows and things like that, work really well in the

You can catch just about anything trolling, including nice halibut like the one shown here.

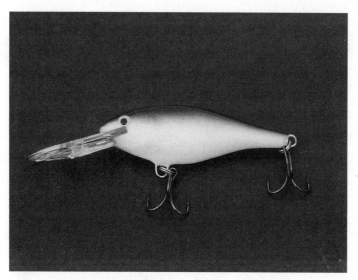

longer-bill (deep-diver) models.

Another good color in hard baits is the rainbow trout. Why that is, I don't know. They love it in both the plastic lures and the hard baits. I like deep divers, and the stick baits, like the Rebel or the Rapala, in the smaller sizes. I like lures that dive

One of the most effective lures I've found for trolling in the bays is the Rapala deep-diver shad, in chrome with a black back.

five feet, ten feet, then I'll use light line and they'll go down fifteen feet or twenty feet when you troll them. The more line you put out behind the boat, the deeper the lure goes. But the best lure that I have found for bays and estuaries is the Bomber model A, in the quarter-ounce in chrome with a black back.

Even when I'm trolling, I use six-pound test. This is where having a smooth drag can be particularly important. Make sure you don't set your drag at more than four pounds, because when a fish hits a trolling lure he hits it hard, and the pull from the boat can make the pressures add up quickly. If you've got a drag that sticks or if it's set too high, the first big fish that chomps your lure is going to snap you right off, and that's not only frustrating, it's expensive.

I like parabolic, graphite rods for trolling as well, and I like them at about six and a half to seven feet in length.

You don't need to set the hook when trolling, as the speed of the boat will do that for you. I like to keep my trolling speed between two and three miles per hour, and that puts plenty of pressure on the line to firmly set the hook. If you keep swinging with your rod, trying to set the hook,

The rainbow trout pattern also catches a lot of fish in the bays, even if I've never seen anything that looks like a rainbow trout in the bays.

you'll lose a lot fish by pulling the lure right out of their mouths, sometimes with their lips still attached. Fish lips don't count as fish caught.

I troll with my lure three to four boat lengths behind the boat; the farther back the lure, the deeper it will dive.

Once my lure's in the water, I hold the rod so it's pointed out to the side of the boat, not over the back.

I then let the lure slowly pull the rod tip toward the back of the boat, until the tip is pointed behind the boat.

Then I bring the rod back to the starting position, which makes the lure dart forward at an increased speed.

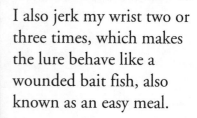

I also jerk my wrist two or three times, which makes the lure behave like a wounded bait fish, also known as an easy meal.

If there's a fish near the lure, or if one has been following it trying to decide whether or not this is lunch, these movements will often entice the fish to strike. Be alert, because when a fish strikes while you're jerking the rod he can take it away from you if you're holding it too loosely. And if a fish takes your rod away, it's a big win for him, and all of his friends will laugh at you.

Land a fish you hooked trolling just like you'd land a fish you caught casting. If he's a big fish, pump him and reel. If he's not, bring him in and let him go.

When you do hook a fish on a crank bait while trolling, don't horse him in. There's no sport in seeing if you can get a small fish to skip across the surface, and a big fish might throw the hook. Once he's on, it really doesn't matter whether you hooked him trolling or casting, so you should bring him in the same way regardless of how you caught him. As always, never give him any slack line.

It's very tempting, when using deep-diver lures, to reach down into the water and pull the fish out by grasping the crankbait and lifting. Don't do it. If the fish somehow throws the hook, it will go from his mouth directly into your hand, and it is no fun to have treble hooks embedded in your hand. When you get the fish to the boat, if you can't bounce him, use the net.

I've said over and over, it's the little things that make the difference. If you do all the little things right, the big things will take care of them-

selves. Like catching a fish.

There's a skipper in San Diego named Buzz Brizendine, who, when he gives seminars says, the two most critical times when you hook a fish are the first ten seconds and the last ten seconds. And nothing could be truer when it comes to fishing.

It's tempting to grab the bill of your deep-diver and hoist the fish into the boat, but that's also a good way to lose the fish and gain a treble hook in your finger. It's always safer to use the net.

In the first ten seconds, you need to set the hook properly, embed the hook in the fish's mouth and have your drag set properly so you don't break the line on the hook set. It's critical. Then, when you've got the fish to the boat, if it's a big fish and they're going to net it and you don't have it in free spool when he nets

it, and the fish flips avoids the net, the line pops, snaps and he's off. But if it's in free spool and your thumb is on the line, he dropped back in the water and you can fight him back up to the net again.

Every area is different, and every method that guys develop has its day. Certain things will work at certain times. My method is a consistent

method that works all the time, and what is most important about my method? Recognizing the fact that the fish is on the other end of the line and once he's there, setting the hook. The lure is in his mouth, not in his hands. *Fish have no hands.*

FINDING 5 THE FISH

We've discussed where to find the fish, what equipment to use and how to use it, so at this point you're set to catch bunches of fish in your local bays and estuaries. But if you want to get the biggest edge possible, let's take a closer look at where you're going to find those fish, why they're there, and when's the best time to catch them.

Being a successful angler requires lots of practice, although in fishing, practice never makes perfect. But it does make fishing much better. It can help you to notice patterns in weather, water conditions and habitat, which will improve your fishing.

Fish are ruled largely by the iron hand of their environment. While they follow certain internal signals such as hunger, survival instincts and reproduction, where they are at any given moment and their willingness to strike a lure are governed mostly by environmental variables. By studying the most important of these variables, we can unlock many secrets of fish behavior, and increase our daily catches.

The most important of these factors are water temperature, oxygen content, light penetration, food supplies and available cover, or structure. The places which have the best combination of these elements will hold the majority of the adult fish, and since these places are the ideal feeding spots for the fish, they should be the ideal catching spots for you.

The more diligent you are in doing your homework, the more successful you'll be. Remember, information and knowledge almost always lead to more fish. So before you make your first cast, gather as much information as you can about each of the above variables, and put it all

together to organize a plan of attack. This can save you a tremendous amount of time. Every day and every area are different, and studying the environmental factors is the surest, fastest way to figure out where the fish are and what it will take to catch them.

Always take the time to study the water and terrain you'll be fishing before you start to fish. A little advance planning can add up to many more fish caught.

Water Temperature

Anglers need to pay close attention to water temperature, because it regulates the fish's bodily functions and metabolism. Each species of fish has a specific temperature range in which his body operates best. Largemouth, freshwater bass, for example, prefer water that is about sixty-six to seventy-five degrees. If the other environmental variables are favorable (and therefore not a factor), bass will actively seek out this ideal temperature range and stay there. However, if the other environmental factors are not favorable, they may leave this comfort zone to adapt. To feed, for instance, or to avoid a poor oxygen region.

Water approximately eight degrees warmer than his ideal is about the maximum a largemouth bass will tolerate for more than a few minutes.

When his shallow water feeding grounds become too warm in the summer months, he'll probably visit them only for a few minutes at a time, and spend the rest of the day in the cooler, deeper water.

These quick visits are possible because it takes about twenty minutes for his body to assume the temperature of the surrounding water, be it warmer or colder. In warm bodies of water, a bass' ideal temperature may rise a few degrees during the summer to compensate for the increase in overall water temperature. If conditions become too severe, bass will usually shut down until they improve. As a rule, the smaller the bass, the less he is affected by water temperatures warmer than his ideal.

In colder months, bodies of fresh water are relatively uniform in temperature. However, from late spring to early fall they usually stratify, creating distinct thermal layers. In salt and fresh water, the warmer upper layers react to weather conditions, such as wind, sun and air temperature, while deeper layers are sealed off, and therefore change little on a thermal basis from day to day.

Sun and air temperature are the two main con-

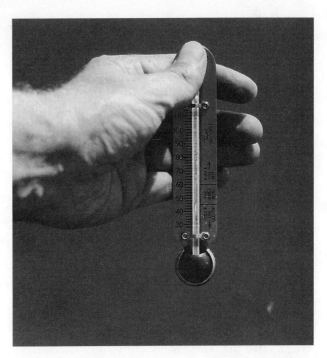

A water thermometer can tell you the exact temperature of the water you're fishing, which can help you to anticipate how active the fish will be, and how they will react to your lures.

tributors of heat and cold to water. The effect of either depends on the wind. When the wind is calm, heat from the sun can fully penetrate into the upper layers of water, causing them to warm as much as ten degrees. When the wind is blowing, on the other hand, wave action scatters this heat back into the air, so little is gained from the sun. But these waves will pull in heat or cold from the air and mix it into the water.

Oxygen Content

Fish have the same moment-to-moment need for oxygen as you and I; they just breathe it differently.

The minimum amount of oxygen required for a bass to be completely comfortable ranges from approximately two to ten parts per million (PPM). It all depends on his size, his present activity, and the temperature of the water around him. For example, a five-pound bass resting in forty degree water needs only five PPM to breathe without stress. On the other extreme, that same bass feeding actively in eighty-five degree water would need at least ten PPM to breathe comfortably, and that's without one of those nose-strip things.

Water gets the vast majority of its oxygen from microscopic plants called plankton. These tiny plants also form the foundation of the food chain. If these organisms are not in abundance, such as during the cooler months of the year, then air is the primary contributor—only at a much slower rate.

Water and air constantly try to stay balanced with each other in regards to oxygen. When water is holding all of the oxygen it can without passing some off to the air, it is said to be in a state of one hundred percent saturation.

Water clarity is also important in how well oxygenated a body of water is, since plankton, silt particles and other minute objects compete with dissolved oxygen for space. So, murky waters are the most susceptible to oxygen problems, especially when air temperatures rise above seventy degrees.

Like clear water, cold water is capable of holding more oxygen, so you really don't need to worry too much about oxygen content until the summer. Oxygen maximums, which are any areas of water containing more oxygen than the water around them, sometime occur around weed beds or kelp on calm, sunny days, where streams feed the bay or ocean after a rain, and along winding shores on cloudy days.

The compensation level is the level where the upper half of a body of water, where oxygen can be replenished by sun and wind, meets the lower half, where oxygen dwindles during the summer. The oxycline is the last depth of water that has enough oxygen to keep fish comfortable in a resting state.

While some of the other variables, like water temperature, are controlling factors, telling fish what to do and when to do it, oxygen is a limiting factor, telling fish whether they can do something, and to what degree. Once the oxygen content drops below a fish's minimum requirement, he'll try to compensate by first trying to find more oxygenated water, then by breathing faster, and then by turning down his metabolism.

If none of these return him to his oxygen comfort zone, he'll then stop feeding, and if that doesn't do it, he'll shut down all non-vital bodily functions, as if in a state of hibernation. And if all of this fails, as a last resort he'll regurgitate the contents of his stomach, since digesting food requires a little extra oxygen intake. At this point, if the oxygen content in the water does not improve within a few hours, the fish will die.

Fortunately, fish will automatically swim out of anoxic water and return to oxygenated water, just as you or I would hold our breath and return to the surface if we fell overboard and into the water. So for a bass to suffocate in the water would require near-cataclysmic events to occur, although they will stay away from anoxic water in droves.

However, there is a much easier way for fish to die of asphyxiation, and it happens all too frequently. As I mentioned in the last chapter, it's not hard to burn up a fish's oxygen supply fighting him to the boat. You can exhaust a fish to the point where he can't swim any more, which means he can't force water through his gills, which means he can't breathe. Imagine if you could get so tired that you couldn't breathe. Very unpleasant. Well fish can get that tired, and often do fighting anglers.

If you don't take that exhausted fish and run his gills through the water a few times and get some oxygen back into him, he's just going to sink and die of oxygen deprivation when you drop him back into the water. It took him years to get to be big enough for you to catch him, and minutes for you to kill him because you didn't release him the proper way. That doesn't make much sense, does it?

LIGHT PENETRATION

Bright light does not hurt, blind or damage the eyes of the fish you'll find near shore and in bays and estuaries. It does, however, threaten their security, making them rather nervous and inducing them to hide from their enemies (like us), either tucking into good cover or heading into deeper water.

It also exposes them to their prey, which they prefer to overcome by ambushing them from good cover and by waiting until low-light periods when they can see much better than their optically challenged lunch.

If you can't see a white lure more than one foot beneath the surface of the water, light penetration will not be a factor in your angling strategy, because there isn't any.

In clearer water, the level of light penetration helps determine how closely a fish relates to objects while resting, and when he will feed. In water with little or no cover, light has a strong influence on the fish's preferred depth, but only if water temperature and oxygen content are not factors.

FOOD SUPPLIES

Rather than haphazardly searching for fish, first locate those things that attract fish in large numbers, and start there.

Bays and harbors are full of man-made structure that fosters life low on the food chain, which then attracts bait fish, which, of course, will then bring around the game fish. Keep an eye on the area around the docks for bait fish activity. The game fish will be close by.

Obviously, one of the most important of these is food.

The food chain is pretty simple: The bait fish eat the plankton, the game fish eat the bait fish. So, the first thing you want to do is find the areas with the highest concentrations of plankton and cover. Light penetration determines the depth at which the plankton can grow, which will bring out the bait fish, which will bring out the game fish. Any depth reading one hundred percent light penetration or better on an angler's light meter will probably support this green, microscopic plant life.

Weed beds, kelp and winding shorelines often hold large concentrations of plankton. Since the food the game fish are looking for—bait fish— also require cover, look for those vast weedy, brushy and rocky areas which lie within the one hundred percent light metered region. If weeds are abundant, the major feeding layer of the fish will usually run from the last depth that has rooted vegetation up to the surface. This layer is called the primary food zone, or, more commonly, the shallows.

When a bass is in the shallows, he's probably feeding. Exceptions would be during the spawning season, during the summer when poor oxygen levels in the deeper water forces him to stay shallow, or when the area has such good shallow water cover that he feels comfortable spending his non-feeding hours there.

Being up and feeding means the bass are scattered, aggressive and more vulnerable to lures. In other words, this is very good for you.

When the fish are below the primary food zone, they're considered to be in deep water and will generally be more schooled, less willing to hit a lure and harder to locate. This transition depth near shore can be anywhere from three to thirty feet, depending on the water clarity and structure in the area.

FISH HAVE NO HANDS

STRUCTURE

Structure is simply submerged objects, such as trees, tires, weeds, engine blocks, pilings, you name it, and irregularities in the contour of the bottom, such as drop-offs, channels and rocks, that fish relate to. In short, it is anything that's different from its surroundings.

The view at low tide reveals one of the reasons fish like structure so much—food. But structure in deeper water, such as these pilings, can be used as reference points by the fish. Road signs on the fish highways, if you will.

Most fish use structure for two main purposes: for reference points to keep themselves oriented, and for cover, to hide from their prey (remember, bass are ambush feeders) and to conceal them from their enemies.

As a rule, fish seek the cover aspect mostly in the shallows, where they encounter both prey and enemies. They use structure more for reference points while they're resting in deeper water or moving from one place to another.

These two uses are the foundation of understanding structure, and should be indelibly stamped into your fish-seeking mind.

Compared to other game fish, near-shore game fish prefer warmer water than most, but this does not mean they all live in the shallows. In fact, their fear of things from "the other world," above the surface, is so ingrained that if the fish had their way, they would stay in the security of the deeper water all of their lives, and if they really had their way, you'd be a duck hunter.

This, of course, is not possible, because almost everything they eat is found in the upper layers, as is their spawning ground. Lucky for you and the ducks. Even if the majority of your fish are caught from shallow water, remember that, in general, most of the time the majority of the bass are where they really prefer to be—in their deep water rest-ing areas.

While fish would probably prefer to spend their time in safer, deeper water, they've got to eat, and most of their food is found in shallower water.

The biggest exception to this is in bodies of water loaded with ideal cover. Even in the extreme shallows, good cover apparently provides all of the security they need, so some fish just stay there all the time, going deeper only when forced to by adverse conditions.

Sometimes called a sanctuary or the fish's home, the outstanding feature of a deep water resting area is its value as a reference point. It doesn't really matter whether it's an object, such as a piling, or an irregularity, like a sudden drop-off; it just has to have some obvious feature the fish can hang around to stay oriented while resting, and recognize when going to or coming from an excursion. If it also provides cover, fine. But that element is not usually necessary—the deep water serves as all the protection the fish feels he needs.

So, if the fish use anything from beer cans to boulders as reference points, what makes them prefer one area over another? Like us, the chicks. No, just kidding. First and foremost, the closer the structure is to a good feeding ground, the better. This cannot be stressed enough. We all like to live close to where we work.

Fish, especially the old-timers, find very little thrill in commuting long distances every time they want to eat. The farther they travel, the more food they need to ingest to make up for the energy expended just getting there. This isn't laziness, it's a matter of survival. Theoretically, a scrawny twig adjacent to a food-infested shallow area would serve as a better home than a large hollow log a mile away.

Next, this structure will be even more attractive to fish if it is in sequence with other reference points leading to a feeding ground. In other words, if it's part of the fish gravy train. A series of these structures will form a highway for the fish to follow going to and from the shallows. One interesting thing to remember is that dirtier the water, the closer together these should be. When a bass is at one structure, he prefers to be able to see the next, rather than strike out blindly and hope he's heading in the right direction. Unlike many anglers I know.

Once you find a good area, chances are it will contain a number of different structures, each meeting these two requirements. While they are all potential fish hangouts, usually your search can be narrowed to just a few. First of all, it is only logical that the larger structures will harbor more fish. A submerged piling may be an excellent reference point, but, because of its size, it may support no more than one or two fish. Also, it would be harder for you to find. A big rock pile, on the other hand, is easier to locate on a depth finder and can handle an entire school of fish.

If a particular piece of structure in shallow water affords a fish everything he wants, namely food and shelter, he may spend most of his time shallow, seeking deeper water only when forced to by adverse conditions.

Fish tend to prefer tall objects or irregularities. Since their ideal depth often shifts up and down, a standing piling or a steep rock bluff means the fish can shift right along with the changes to his environment and still keep relating to the same reference point. The taller structures are perennial fish resting areas for just that reason.

Even though most of the time the fish are in deep water, those that are shallow are considerably more catchable. With the exceptions of spawning and being forced up by poor oxygen, a shallow fish is a feeding fish, and is therefore more likely to crunch a lure and add to your catch count.

There is definite merit in learning what fish demand from structure while visiting the shallows. As stated earlier, this is mainly cover. To conceal them from prey and enemies, and just like deep water reference points, just any old structure won't do.

Rule number one, of course, is that the cover must be among food. Fish know what type of prey offers the most nutrition, and they know where to find it. Usually it's around dense, fine-stemmed structures, like weeds, eel grass, kelp and rock piles. These provide the prey with protection from the game fish. When threatened, the smaller fish can dart into the tiny openings where the larger predators can't follow. Vast rocky areas can also be good, for the same reasons.

The second rule—less strict, but important nonetheless—is that cover should offer the game fish good concealment. His favorite tactic is ambushing, so he needs a spot where the prey has trouble seeing him, plus where a fast exit, to either zap his dinner or flee from danger, is possible.

For example, the outer edge of a weed bed would fulfill both prerequisites, whether the fish lie up against it to wait for something wandering too far out of the weeds, or lie just inside, ready to nail a victim swimming past. The same could hold true for a brush pile or the top end of a fallen tree.

In any of these cases, the cover blends in with the fish's natural coloration, and makes him more difficult to see. The other camouflage trick he uses is to simply hang in a shadow. Most types of bait fish see well in normal bright light, but poorly in anything less. Therefore, something lurking in the shadow of a stump, log or big rock would go virtually unnoticed by the bait fish, until that shadow ate him. But even then, he'd only see him for a second.

One exception to this is when fish feed around rock beds and rocky points. The bait fish and crabs they seek are usually obtained simply by uprooting the stones, so there is no need for concealment on the fish's part.

While some structure would seem to provide less camouflage for fish than others, fish often just hide in the shadows, depending on the poorer vision and inattention of their prey to provide them with their meal.

Finally, the better shallow water ambushing locations will be on or very near a major travel route of bait fish, particularly in areas where bait fish are the main food source. Roaming a lot during daytime, bait fish need highways just like game fish, and they often take rest stops around various structures they encounter. The most obvious, most used and certainly the most common travel route is the shoreline.

Rocky points and jetties provide many hiding places for fish, as well as many sources of food. Game fish often find their prey by uprooting the rocks on the bottom.

In areas with heavy vegetation, it would be the weedline. In many larger areas, where weeds are not predominant but rocks are, shallow channels run a close second to the shoreline. But keep in mind that the extreme shallows are the home of most bait fish.

FISH WHEN THE FISH ARE

If time were no object, most anglers I know would be out fishing all day, every day, pretty much dawn to dusk. They all like to catch fish, but they all like just being out fishing, too.

Unfortunately, in the real world, things like work and family intrude on our full-time fishing schedules, so we need to pick and choose the times we can get our lines in the water.

Since scheduling is already a concern, why not add a few more factors to your decision making process and get the most out of the days you fish? In fact, if you pick your spots correctly, you may find yourself catching more fish in a three- to four-hour period than you used to catch in a full day, especially if you are able to master my technique.

If the number of days you can get out fishing is limited, I strongly recommend picking your fishing days based on the best tides of the month, and pick your time of day around the best tide times for that day.

Most newspapers will print daily and weekly tide information, there are a number of free tide books available at tackle shops, and there are a few more specialized publications that break fishing conditions down even more. If you live in the Southern California area, I highly recommend ordering a copy of *Fishing the Average Tide* by Lou Smitzer (available from Mr. Smitzer at 619/582-1594) and learning how to use it.

Fish are very predicable in their eating habits. If you follow the tide charts and fish the most favorable days, you'll catch more fish.

I do not schedule guide trips for my clients without consulting this book first, because it tells me what I can expect to catch from one day to the next. Of course, certain weather conditions can turn what should be great days into lousy ones. A cold front, for instance, with north or northwest winds, will kill the bite and turn your fishing trip into a boating outing.

Rain doesn't have to be a bad thing, since it's not raining where the fish are, but any sudden change in barometric pressure, which often accompanies rain storms, will shut the bite off.

However, no weather condition will turn what should be lousy days into great days. That doesn't mean that occasionally you may have a great day when you're not supposed to, but it's not going to happen that often. Follow the charts and pick the best days to go out, and your overall results will improve dramatically.

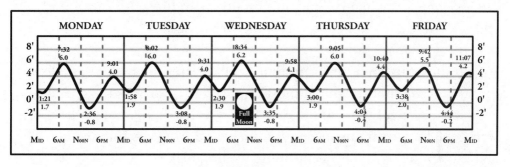

Most newspapers print daily tide charts that show when high tide will occur and how high it will be, and when low tide will occur and how low it will be. The variance is the difference between high tide and low tide, so you would figure that out by adding the high tide and low tide figures together, remembering to change the low tide value from negative to positive or positive to negative, since it's expressed in relation to zero, and not the high tide. For example, the low tide to high tide cycle beginning Wednesday morning at 2:30 at 1.9' and ending at 8:34 at 6.2' would have a variance of 4.3', while the following high to low tide cycle that started at 8:34 at 6.2' and ended at 3:35 at -0.8 has a variance of 7.0'. The greater the variance, the greater the water movement.

As I've said, moving water means feeding fish, and the more water that's moving, the more fish will be feeding. In bays and estuaries, tidal movement is particularly important, as the incoming tide stirs up the bottom and sweeps in small crabs and other such tidbits, and the outgoing tide moves all of this material back the other way.

Both conditions are good for fishing, but I prefer the incoming tide slightly to the outgoing tide. I think the bite's a little better because of the new food it introduces into the bay. Larger game fish will also move into the bays with the incoming tide, gaining access to areas that would otherwise be too shallow for them at lower tide.

During the course of the month there are two types of tides, the spring tide and the neap tide. The spring tide occurs with the full and new moons, which is when the sun and moon are in line with each other, and the two exert their combined pull on the oceans.

As you might imagine, this combined pull creates the highest and lowest tides of the month which, most importantly, provides the greatest variance between high and low tide. The greater this variance, the more water will be moving in and out of the bays during the tide changes, and more moving water means more feeding fish.

The spring tides are always the best time of the month to fish, and some months will be better than others, based on the variance between high tide and low tide.

The other type of tide is the neap tide, which occurs on the first and third quarter phases of the moon, when the sun and moon are at right angles to each other, and their pull on the ocean work at odds with each other. The neap tides produce the lowest variances between high and low tides, which means less moving water and fewer feeding fish.

FISH HAVE NO HANDS

So, if you can only go fishing a day or two each month, you want to plan your trip during a spring tide, and not a neap tide, to take advantage of the greater tide variances and higher number of feeding fish.

New Moon	**First Quarter**	**Full Moon**	**Third Quarter**
Spring Tide	**Neap Tide**	**Spring Tide**	**Neap Tide**

The phase of the moon will determine the activity of the tides. Spring tides, which are the best tides of the month, occur during the full and new moon phases. Neap tides occur during the first and third quarter phases.

Okay, so now you're going out on a spring tide day, but maybe you've only got three or four hours before duty calls, and then you have to be back to the shore. What time do you go?

Look at your tide chart for the day, and find which tide will have the greatest variance between high and low, or maybe, low and high. The times listed are for the absolute low and high tides, which is known as the slack tide. The slack tide is a period of almost no water movement, because the tide is shifting from going in to going out, or vice-versa, and at some point it's got to stop. This is that point. But it also takes some time, after the current stops, for the water to start moving in the other direction and to get up to speed.

If you break up the time between low tide and high tide into quarters, you can easily determine when the fish should start to bite, and when the bite will taper off. It takes about one quarter of the time between high and low tide for the water to get moving to a point where the fish will start to feed.

At this point, when you're one-quarter of the way into the tide cycle, the speed, or velocity, of the current is seventy percent of its maximum. When you're halfway through the tide cycle, current velocity is at one hundred percent, or as fast as it's going to get, and when you're three-quarters of the way through the tide cycle, current velocity will be back to seventy percent, and dropping.

The best time to fish is between the first and third quarters of this cycle, with the best fishing happening right in the middle when the water is moving as fast as it can. Once current velocity drops below that seventy percent level, you're getting into the slack tide range, and the bite will drop off, or even shut off.

If you've got all day, this is a good time to eat your lunch or do some sightseeing. But if you've only got a few hours, you've already been out for the best part of the fishing day, so pack up your gear and head in happy.

WEDNESDAY

The geography of bays and estuaries will affect the speed of the incoming and outgoing tides in certain areas, and by recognizing these areas you can locate where the fish are most likely to be.

The first and last twenty-five percent of a tide cycle provides the poorest water movement, and the slowest fishing. Try to target the middle fifty percent, when the water is moving at its fastest and the bite is at its best.

For example, when the same volume of water that passes through a wide channel or large area passes through a narrower channel, water velocity increases. Essentially, this is more moving water. So look at your bay, and note where the channel narrows. If it's by the mouth, this is usually a particularly good spot, because all of the bait fish washed in and out of the bay by the current must pass right by, and if you're fishing there, right by your lure.

Just like in freshwater rivers and streams, any outcropping on the bay shore or bend in the channel will cause the current to swirl away, resulting in an eddy of slow-moving water on the down current side, which is a favorite place for game fish to hang out, waiting for hapless bait fish who are caught in the rapidly swirling water to be tossed their way.

Look around your bay again. What's in the way of the current, and what could be creating these little pockets of game fish-in-waiting?

We've talked about structure, and why fish like it, but structure also has an effect on current, especially if it's big, man-made structure like pilings and bridges, which are quite common in most bays.

Fishing when the water movement is at its greatest will increase your chances for a big day.

When the current hits a bridge support, for instance, it has to split to go around it, which increases the current velocity, a good thing. Then, when it converges on the other side of the obstacle, one of those bait fish-trapping, game fish hangout eddys occur. Yet another good thing. And on top of it all, these structures usually have plant and animal life growing on them, such as algae and mussels and such, which qualifies as a food source. Mental note— try around the bridge the next time out.

If you can get out on the bay during an extreme low tide, take note of

the holes and structure exposed, and then apply what you know about fish habits to help plan your fishing strategy for when the tide rises. The more you think, the

Bridges provide more fishing opportunity than most structure, as their supports are large enough to disrupt the current and form bait fish-trapping eddies behind them. Follow the water movement, and cast your lure behind the supports, into the eddies.

more you learn, and the more you know, all increase the number of fish you catch.

Working your lure, feeling the pressure bite, setting the hook; all of these are critical to your fishing success, but using your head in deciding when and where to apply your technique and expertise will create a dynamite fish catching combination.

Remember what I said way back at the beginning? There are no big secrets. It's all a matter of doing the little things right. The more little things you do right, the better you'll do.

There is no big secret to being a successful angler—it's all in doing the little things right. Use the right equipment, learn to sense the pressure bite, set the hook immediately and don't give him slack line, fish where the fish are and when the fish are feeding; these are just some of the little things that will increase your catch count on a regular basis.

THE LAST WORD

Whenever I finish a guide trip, I turn to my customers and ask, "Okay, what have you learned today?" So I guess that question is now for you. What have you learned today?

Well, the first thing you should have learned is that *fish have no hands.* That little teeny tightening of the line, that little tick, that you thought was the lure hitting the bottom, was a strike. The fish had the lure in his mouth. If you waited to set the hook, you missed the fish. So the most important thing to remember is to set the hook immediately, and reel while you swing. If you don't reel instantaneously, you will miss most of your strikes.

We've also talked about the importance of using the right equipment, and taking care of it. You will get bit far more often using six-pound test than you will using eight- or ten-pound test, and you should make sure you're using a high-quality, abrasion-resistant line. Your line is the only link between you and the biggest fish you've caught in your life, so spend the extra money and get the good stuff.

Match your light line to the appropriate tackle. A good, light action, parabolic, graphite rod really does the job for bay and estuary fishing. As I've said, I'm particular to the Lamiglas Mike Gardner In-Shore Pro rod line, because they made them to my specifications.

Lamiglas did a bunch of technical stuff involving things like first generation graphite and improved resin systems, but it's easiest to just say the rods have great action, and cast well both in open water and when I'm casting tight up into structure. For my kind of fishing, I couldn't ask for a better rod.

You can fish my method with spinning reels or baitcasters, but you'll do a whole lot better with a baitcaster, because it will give you a much better feel for your line, and you'll notice the little pressure bites much easier. If you're resisting using a baitcaster because you're worried about backlashes when you cast, don't sweat it. The casting controls on most baitcasters will let you adjust the reels to a point where you can cast without a backlash nearly every time, and you can work your way into longer casts with less casting control as you educate your thumb.

Make long casts up current, because the fish will be looking that way, waiting for an easy meal to come rolling along. When your lure looks like an easy meal, which it should, you'll get bit.

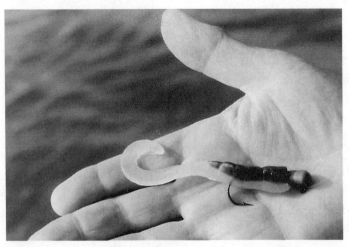

I've told you which lures are the most effective in the bays, harbors and estuaries, and that my favorites are AA's single curly tail and shad in chartreuse and gold. Make sure you use the right lead head with the right lure, and that you assemble them properly.

Keep your hooks sharp, and check them regularly. You'll be amazed at the difference a sharp hook can make when you're setting the hook on a pressure bite, and if you don't get him, at least you'll know you've done everything you could.

Be sure to check your lure every time you bring it in, and remove any debris it may have picked up on the way in. You're fishing along the bottom, and it's very easy to pick up all manner of junk on your lure. There's no point in casting a lure with garbage on it, because no fish is going to take it.

The vibration of your lure is critical, so if anything happens to the lure that will change its vibration, like getting the tail bitten off, change the lure. Again, there's no point casting a lure that won't vibrate correctly, so don't

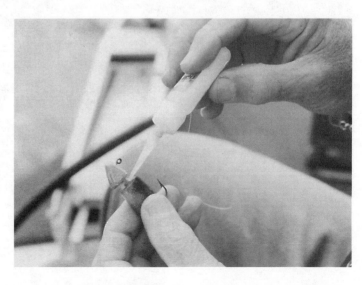

think you're saving any time and getting in more fishing than you would if you stopped to change your lure. You're not getting in more fishing, you're just getting in more casting.

Always fish where the fish are. The number one reason I catch more fish than nearly anyone else is that I'm fishing where the fish are almost all of the time. I'll use every bit of knowledge I have about bays, harbors and estuaries, how the fish behave, and what attracts them or chases them away. I'll also use my electronics to their fullest capabilities. You could be the best angler in the world, master my technique and fish everyday, but if you're not fishing where the fish are, you won't catch fish. It's that simple.

Keep in mind that moving water means feeding fish. If you're in a spot where you know there are fish but you're not getting bit because there's not enough water movement, try another spot and come back when the

tide's picked up. Or eat your lunch. There's no guarantee that no fish will hit your lure during a slack or slow tide, but it's certain that you'll get more strikes as the amount of moving water increases.

Learn to read the tide charts, and plan your fishing days according to the best tides. Of course, the worst day of fishing really is better than the best day of working, so if the choice is simply whether or not to go fishing, I'm all for going. But if you only have so many days you can fish, pick the ones with the best tides and highest variances, to give you the best chances for catching fish.

Fish relate to structure, so you should always be fishing on or near structure. Don't forget that structure also applies to underwater terrain, such as ledges, drop-offs and submerged pilings. This is where good electronics can give you an even greater edge in finding fish.

One of the most common problems I find with people learning to recognize a pressure strike is that they can't get past their preconceived notions of what a bite feels like. I can tell them over and over about pulling their shirt one-quarter inch away from their chest, but they still think they'll know a bite when they feel it. The more experienced the angler, the more trouble I have with this.

I was out recently with a customer who was a professional salmon guide, and a buddy of his who just liked to fish. I explained the pressure bite to the two of them, and the buddy got it right away but the guide didn't. The buddy and I were catching all kinds of fish, but the guide wasn't catching a thing. He was getting bit, but he just didn't recognize the pressure bites.

His buddy and I chided him unmercifully, and he said, "Don't you think I know when I'm getting bit? I'm a professional guide. I teach people how to fly fish for salmon. Don't you think I know when I'm bit?"

And we kept telling him that he was waiting for the lure to take off, for a rip-roaring strike, and that it just wasn't going to happen. The buddy and I were getting bit on the sink; the fish would take it, and the lure would just stop sinking. No crashing strike. No peeling off of the drag. The lure would just stop sinking, because the fish had it in his mouth. We'd set the hook, and catch a fish.

Of course, you have to pay attention. He was busy talking—we were all telling each other stories—and he wasn't paying that much attention. He still thought he was going to get that big strike.

It took him an hour and a half to catch his first fish, and by that time his buddy and I had already pulled at least ten fish each into the boat. Needless to say, he was getting a little frustrated.

But toward the end of the day he finally figured it out, and was able to ignore what he'd always thought a bite felt like. Then he caught fire. After all, he *was* a professional fisherman, and once he'd realized what a bite felt like, he was hauling them in one after another. We must have caught two hundred fish that day, even with the salmon guide sandbagging it for the first half of the day.

When we got back in, he said, "You know, if someone had told me before this trip that I didn't know what it felt like to get bit with a pressure bite, I would've laughed at 'em." Turned out, the laugh was on him.

Another time I was out with a bass fisherman, a guy who has his own bass boat, and this guy's daughter, who'd just graduated from college. She kicked his butt. He's a member of a bass club, and she just mopped the floor with him. Why?

Because he had a preconceived idea of what it felt like to have a bass hit a plastic lure, and was waiting for that tap-tap, that tug-tug, that thunk-thunk, which very rarely came. She listened when I explained about what a pressure bite was, and when she felt it, she set the hook and reeled. She was catching fish right and left.

She was willing to listen and learn, but her dad, the bass fisherman, thought he knew all he needed to know about how a bass strike feels, and the pressure strike concept couldn't get past what he already knew. He didn't have such a hot day. She had a blast, though.

How well you do fishing my method will depend greatly on how quickly you learn to recognize the pressure strike. If you're hard-headed, and believe you already know what a bite feels like, you struggle for a while. If you're patient, and take the time to master the feeling of the pressure strike, you'll be amazed at the number of fish you'll catch.

Now all through this book, we've talked about huge numbers of fish you can catch in a day, and I've caught those big numbers many times

myself, and continue to catch them. But I can't stress enough the importance of practicing proper catch and release techniques.

If you catch one hundred fish in a day, and half of them die after you release them because you didn't handle them properly, you'll deplete a bay very quickly, and all because of carelessness.

It takes many years for bay species to replenish themselves, and if you decimate a fish population, it could be a long time before you catch a large number of fish again. It also takes quite a few years for most fish to reach any decent size, and it's years of struggle and toil, so don't waste it by needlessly killing a fish. If you intend to eat him for dinner, fine. If you're just going to take him home to show someone that you caught him, throw him back. Your ego's not that fragile, I hope.

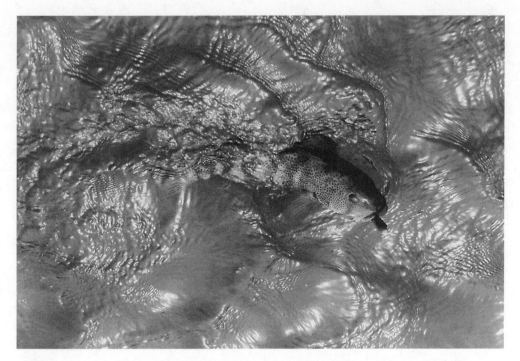

Also, whatever you take out onto the bay should go back with you. Nothing goes in the water except your lure and the fish. No cigarette or cigar butts, no paper, no trash, no cans, no bottles. Particularly no bottles. Any time I see someone throw a bottle in the water, I get really angry. It's too easy for some kid to step on that bottle, and severely cut his foot.

I lost a bass tournament one time, when I jumped in the water to cool off and stepped on a bottle. I had the tournament won with the fish in my live well, but instead of weighing in, I was on my way to the emergency room. Anyone who throws a bottle off my boat goes in after it.

It's up to the responsible anglers to remind the irresponsible anglers that they're out of line. The harbor patrol can't be everywhere at once, and if you see someone throwing junk in the water, it's very easy to give them a casual reminder that they dropped something. You don't have to be confrontational or belligerent, just polite.

If someone is really crossing the line, say, dumping fuel or oil in the bay, just jot down their boat registration number and pass it on to the harbor patrol. No one should get away with that kind of behavior.

I've been told, "You're only as good as the best fisherman you know," and I believe that wholeheartedly. If you're out all of the time by yourself, or with the same guys over and over, you're not learning all that much. Information almost always leads to more fish. Talk to as many good anglers as you can, and seek out good information wherever you can find it.

Read other fishing books, subscribe to fishing magazines that cover the type of fishing you like to do, go to fishing seminars and attend the big fishing shows in your area. The shows can be particularly helpful, because not only do they attract a tremendous amount of anglers, both amateur and professional, the tackle manufacturers are also there in

force, and you'll find out the latest on both equipment and techniques.

There is a wealth of good information available out there, and you never know when one little nugget you picked up in a magazine article will turn what would have been a lousy day into a good day of fishing.

Remember, anyone can catch fish when the bite's wide open and the fish will take potatoes tied to rope. It takes a real fisherman to catch fish when the bite's off, or the fish are being particularly finicky.

You can never learn enough. Every time you go fishing, you should be learning a little more that will make you just that much better an angler. Fishing is like a puzzle, and it's up to you to figure out the answers. You now have a lot more information than you did before, but that doesn't guarantee that you'll have a great day every time you go out.

Never fall into the trap of thinking you know everything there is to know about fishing. I've been doing this all of my life, and I'm constantly learning new things. You should be too.

So the next time you're out on the bay, practicing my method, and wondering what that funny little tick is on the end of the line, SET THE HOOK! Because if you learned nothing else in these pages, you should at least know that *fish have no hands*.

TALKING THE TALK

There are thousands of terms anglers use to describe what they do and the things involved. An exhaustive list would be enough to fill another book, so I'll include just a few of my favorites.

AUXILIARY—The small, electric powerplant aboard a boat which generates and supplies electrical power to the craft.

BARNDOOR—A very large halibut, usually one more than twenty pounds.

BLANK—The tubular shaft portion of a fishing rod. A blank typically can be constructed of fiberglass, boron, graphite or a combination of these materials. Blank also means to catch nothing, as in, "It was really slow today. He was blanked, and I only caught fifty fish."

BREEZERS—School game fish that are on or near the surface and swimming rapidly, either during migrations or when chasing forage fish.

BLIND STRIKE—A strike on a bait or a lure unseen by the angler, usually referring to trolling.

COFFEE GRINDER—An open-face spinning reel.

DEADHEAD—A non-paying angler, usually a guest, on a party boat.

DUSTED—Used when describing losing a fish, usually a big one (are small fish ever lost?), following a long, powerful and uncontrollable run by the fish.

FOLLOWER—A fish that follows or chases your lure during your retrieve, or while trolling, but doesn't take it, darn it. Sometimes called a shadower, a tracker, or an annoying fish that just won't take your lure.

GRUMP—A big fish.

LONG RELEASE—Face-saving term for losing a fish while he's still far from the boat. Much more efficient and time-saving than catch and release, but not quite as much fun.

MEATBALL—A school or ball of bait fish, such as anchovies or smelt, pushed to the surface and herded together by attacking game fish. A very good sign.

MEMORY—Referring to monofilament line, its ability to remember or forget the abuse it's received in the course of fishing. In this case, you want the worst memory possible.

PILGRIM—A rookie fisherman.

RAT—Very small fish.

SHORT—Fish that are smaller than the established legal length limit for that species.

SMOKER—A fast running fish. Also an annoying passenger who wants to stink up your boat and throw his butts in the water.

THROWING IRON—Casting and retrieving artificial lures.

WEEDLINE—The area along the shore where the weeds end and clearer, more open water begins. Usually a good place to throw a lure.

ABOUT THE AUTHOR

Mike Gardner, a well-known bass fisherman and fishing guide, is on the pro or field testing research teams of a number of tackle manufacturers, including Quantum, Stren and Lamiglas, who have developed an entire line of Mike Gardner In-Shore Pro fishing rods.

Mike also participates in extensive biological research regarding in-shore, bay and estuary fish species for the Department of Fish and Game. He has made numerous radio and television appearances, is a regular contributor to a variety of fishing publications, and appears in his own bass fishing video that demonstrates his personal technique for fishing near shore, in bays and estuaries.

Introducing the

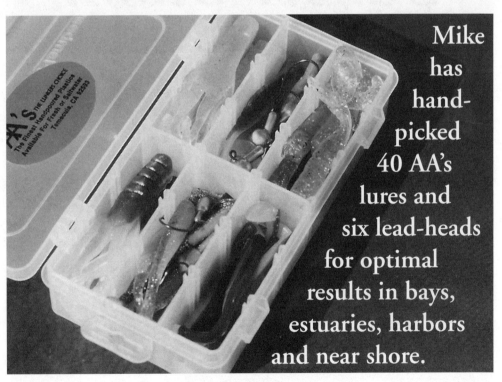

South Coast Sportfishing

The 3-Minute Subscription.

It's Completed Faster than a Giant Tuna can Empty a Tiny Spinning Reel.

Subscribe the Easy Way to
South Coast Sportfishing:
Phone Us at (714) 258-2344
Fax Us at (714) 258-3448
Charge a 1- or 2-Year Subscription
on Your VISA, MasterCard or AMEX
FAST! EASY! CONVENIENT!

Hook Up With *SCS* Today!

Go Fishing With
Mike Gardner

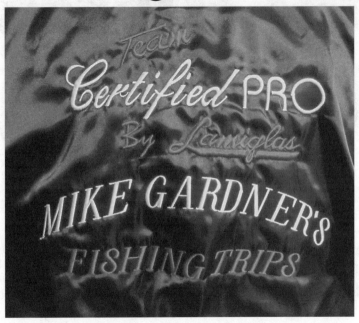

If you live in Southern California or plan a visit, be sure to book a trip with the master himself.
See Mike's technique demonstrated up close and personal, and learn more about fishing in a day than you may have learned in a lifetime!

Call and book your trip today.

Licensed   **714/671-0447**   Bonded